OVER AFRICAN JUNGLES

Books by Martin Johnson

SAFARI

LION

CONGORILLA

OVER AFRICAN JUNGLES

SUNSET. Sunset on Lake Naivasha, British East Africa. The African savages watched in wonder this flying home of the white people, who could live in the air, on water and on land. As there are many lakes in Central and East Africa, our amphibians were invaluable for exploration work.

Over African Jungles

BY MARTIN JOHNSON

THE RECORD OF A GLORIOUS ADVENTURE
OVER THE BIG GAME COUNTRY OF AFRICA
60,000 MILES BY AIRPLANE

WITH 100 PHOTOGRAPHS

HARCOURT, BRACE AND COMPANY

NEW YORK

PRINTED IN THE UNITED STATES OF AMERICA
BY QUINN & BODEN COMPANY, INC., RAHWAY, N. J.
Typography by Robert Josephy

DEDICATION

As all books seem to need dedication, it seems fitting that this one should be dedicated to Adventure, without which Osa and I would never be happy. Adventure has been our object in a lifetime of seeking the unusual, the unknown, and, with all, the wonderful feeling of freedom.

We hope that this volume will interest and thrill those who are not so fortunate as we who are able to make our business our pleasure . . . always seeking the pot of gold at the foot of the rainbow, and never finding it; but then, we don't care; it's a life of Glorious Adventure that we seek and find.

ILLUSTRATIONS

Illustrations

Illustrations

Illustrations

OVER AFRICAN JUNGLES

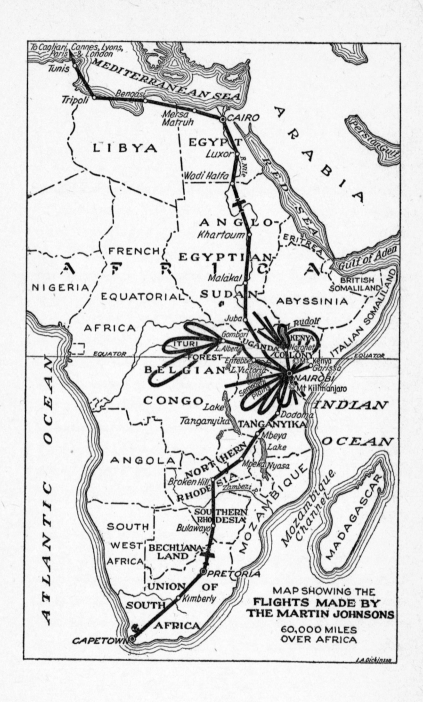

To Cagliari, Cannes, Lyons, Paris & London

Tunis

MEDITERRANEAN SEA

Tripoli
Bengasi
Mersa Matruh
CAIRO

LIBYA   EGYPT
Luxor
R. Nile
Wadi Halfa

ARABIA

Persian Gulf

RED SEA

ANGLO-
Khartoum
EGYPTIAN
SUDAN
Malakal

ERITREA

Gulf of Aden

BRITISH SOMALILAND

ABYSSINIA

FRENCH

NIGERIA

EQUATORIAL

AFRICA

A F R I C A

ITALIAN SOMALILAND

Juba
L. Rudolf
EQUATOR   EQUATOR

ITURI
FOREST
Gombari
L. Albert
Entebbe
L. Victoria
UGANDA
KENYA
COLONY
Nakuru
Mt. Kenya
Garissa
NAIROBI
Mt. Kilimanjaro

BELGIAN

CONGO
Lake
Tanganyika

Serengeti Plains

Dodoma

INDIAN

TANGANYIKA
Mbeya
Lake

OCEAN

ANGOLA

NORTHERN

Broken Hill
RHODESIA
Zambezi

Mpeka Nyasa

MOZAMBIQUE

Mozambique Channel

MADAGASCAR

SOUTHERN
RHODESIA
Bulawayo

SOUTH

WEST

AFRICA

BECHUANA-
LAND

UNION   OF
Kimberly

SOUTH   AFRICA

PRETORIA

MAP SHOWING THE
FLIGHTS MADE BY
THE MARTIN JOHNSONS
60,000 MILES
OVER AFRICA

ATLANTIC OCEAN

CAPETOWN

I.A.Dickinson

I

IN THE last fifteen years Osa and I have taken five photographic expeditions to Africa. Others had preceded us, of course—Kearton, Dugmore, and Akeley were some of them—but we have exposed miles of motion picture film in our search for African animal photographs, and even though we were not exactly pioneers in the game, we have seen it progress from the "old" days of safaris on foot, through the automobile era, and well into the era of safaris by air.

The method of going into the field on foot was highly perfected when we first reached Africa in 1920, and we followed in the footsteps of those who had preceded us. Scores of porters, gunbearers, personal "boys," askaris, cooks, and all the rest made up our first safari, and off we went, into "the blue," at the breath-taking rate of ten or fifteen or twenty miles a day—or possibly thirty when the going was especially easy.

But automobiles were already beginning to prove themselves in the rough going about the roadless plains, so we invested in a fleet of cars, and found, to our immense satisfaction, that we could cover much greater distances than ever before, with the expenditure of much less time and energy, and could, as well, carry our supplies with far fewer native "boys" to clutter up the countryside. But having reached the era of automobile safaris, we imagined that the ultimate had been attained, and having played our part in developing the most practical methods of using motor cars in the field, we assumed that so long as we continued to spend our time in such a pursuit we would continue to trust to these rough-riding, but reasonably dependable, vehicles.

And then, after our return from our fourth expedition, I—against my "better judgment"—was forced to make a hurried trip by air. I didn't care for the idea in the least. The great void that I had often noticed between a flying plane and the hard earth over which it was passing seemed so lacking in handholds and parking places in case of trouble. But somehow, the very moment the roaring motors had swept the big transport plane free of the smooth runway at the airport, I developed an entirely new point of view. All sense of risk instantly disappeared, and before the trip was over I was a confirmed enthusiast, intent on learning to fly myself. At that stage in the game the thought of taking my own planes with me to Africa had not begun to take shape, but as I learned to fly—and especially as I inveigled Osa into learning—all sorts of new notions began to develop, with the result that when the "City of New York" ended her voyage from New York to Cape Town in Table Bay, on January 23, 1933, two big planes, with their wings detached, formed the most conspicuous part of her deck cargo, and furthermore, those two planes were ours.

4

OUR PLANES OVER AFRICA. "Osa's Ark" and the "Spirit of Africa," our two beautiful and efficient Sikorsky Amphibians. They flew more than 60,000 miles over East and Central Africa; then up the Nile, across the Mediterranean, across Europe to London. Now, back in America, they are doing perfect work. And Vern Carstens did a marvelous job of keeping them in perfect condition.

NAIROBI FROM THE AIR. A more modern and beautiful little city could not be found any place on earth. It now has excellent theaters, hotels, stores, and municipal buildings. But when we first saw it, it was a city of tin shanties.

Over African Jungles

It is not to be supposed that the organization of a photographic expedition that intends to spend a year and half, or so, in the wilder portions of so vast a continent as Africa is exactly a simple matter. Even the preparations for our earlier expeditions were quite complicated enough. Snapping a kodak in the park or on the beach on Sunday afternoon is so distantly related to making motion pictures of elephants in Kenya, or lions in Tanganyika, as not to be related at all. But if the preparations for making motion pictures require work, that became doubly true when motion picture audiences began to demand sound with their pictures. If I had had to learn how to operate sound equipment when I first took up motion picture photography, I am inclined to think that I would have chosen some simpler job, such as brick laying, perhaps. I had learned a bit about a motion picture camera by the time sound equipment appeared, and though it looked terrible to me, I buckled down and learned a bit about that too. But now, as if these two weren't enough, both Osa and I had learned to fly, and had brought two huge Sikorsky amphibians out to Africa with us in order, no less, that our task might be "simplified."

Now in the old days—that is, in 1920 and for a time thereafter—Osa and I were the whole expedition. Of course, we had porters and cooks and gunbearers and camera bearers, until their numbers more or less equaled that of a company of infantry, but they were servants, to whom our word was law. But now, with cameras (plenty of them, too, with nearly fifty thousand dollars' worth of lenses), sound equipment, and two big airplanes, Osa and I alone would have been far beyond our depth, if that is a proper metaphor to use in relation to such a conglomeration of mechanical gadgets.

The result was that we required help, intelligent help. So, when Osa and I landed at Cape Town, and watched the derricks hoist our planes onto the quay, we were accompanied by six others without whom no such attempt as ours could possibly have succeeded.

Our party, then, in addition to ourselves, consisted of Vern Carstens and Boris Sergievsky, both remarkably able fliers; Al Morway, an airplane mechanic from the Sikorsky factory; Arthur Sanial and Robert Moreno, who were to have charge of the complexities of our sound equipment; and Hugh Davis, who was to be my laboratory man. Certainly we had progressed far from the foot safari days of 1920.

But let no one imagine that two grand airplanes and six grand associates such as these made it possible for us to reach Nairobi, far to the north and east, with no trouble beyond starting the motors. As a matter of fact, it took us two hectic, troublesome, tiring, expensive weeks before we were ready to start our motors and climb into our planes for the take-off. Most of the difficulties and delays were due, it is true, to South African red tape, but they were difficulties and delays, for all that. And expense—why, they charged me more than five hundred dollars for letting the planes stay on the quay for twenty-four hours, and though the other charges were not quite in that proportion, few of them were remarkable because of their modest size.

But I must not enlarge on such unromantic details, for we were about to begin what was, for us, the most marvelously thrilling expedition it has been our privilege to lead in twenty years or more of fascinating expedition work.

If you should get out a map and measure the distance from Cape Town, in South Africa, to Nairobi, in Kenya Colony, you would probably reach the conclusion that the distance is in the neighborhood of 3,600 miles, but you would be mistaken. "As the crow flies" that is, perhaps, fairly accurate, but even a crow doesn't fly "as the crow flies," and overladen Sikorsky amphibians, with insatiable appetites for gasoline, forever have a weather eye open not merely for landing fields, but for landing fields at which their own particular variety of airplane "petrol" can be had. And when one recalls that Africa is second only to Asia in size, and that the interior is not exactly comparable to the states of the Mississippi Valley, one can see that one's air route is not likely to be as straight as the proverbial string. The result of all this was that instead of flying 3,600 miles, we had to fly 4,400 to get to Nairobi, which, thereafter, was to serve as our main base during the coming year and a half. And again, while flying over South Africa was not likely to be very different from flying over portions of the United States, we had then to fly over Bechuanaland, Northern and Southern Rhodesia, a corner of the Belgian

7

Congo, Tanganyika Territory, and Kenya Colony, which is not quite the same as flying over Ohio, Indiana, and Illinois, either in distance or in character of country.

But the big day arrived, and Vern and Boris said we were all ready for the first hop. To Osa and me, it was the thrill of our lives, and our ships were a joy to behold. We had had the big ten-place plane, which I had named "Osa's Ark," painted with the markings of a zebra, while the five-place plane, called the "Spirit of Africa," had been decorated in the manner of a giraffe, and both were as spick and span as when they had left the factory.

We took off from the Cape Town airport at daybreak— Osa and I in the big plane with Captain Sergievsky at the controls, and with Davis and Morway for additional passengers. Vern Carstens piloted the smaller ship, with Moreno and Sanial for company. Moreno holds a private pilot's license and so was able to relieve Carstens from time to time, and Osa and I both could do the same for Sergievsky.

But within twenty minutes things began to happen, and before we reached Nairobi we had been through many things in addition to 4,400 miles of quiet African air.

South Africa is, of course, a highly civilized and a well-developed country, but it is rough and mountainous as well. Down in the southeast, over which, thank goodness, we did not have to fly, the mountains reach an altitude of 10,000 or 11,000 feet, but elsewhere the highest points are not more than 8,000 or 9,000 feet. By great, irregular, terrace-like steps these mountains lead up from the coast to the vast

LANDING STRIP. One of the many landing strips we made during the two years of our Aerial Safari. Though the ground was good for landing, it was almost always dangerous to land here because of treacherous air currents. Conflicting winds from down the valley would drive the "wind sock" around the compass within a few hours.

THE MOST WONDERFUL SIGHT WE SAW. Thousands upon thousands of elephants in herds of from a hundred to five hundred. They were on migration, making their way to the Lorian Swamp, after their regular feeding grounds had dried up. At the Lorian Swamp there is always water and a certain amount of swamp grass to tide them over until the next rains when they will all scatter again.

tableland of the interior which, in the Transvaal, stands a full 6,000 feet above the sea, and within a few hundred miles of Cape Town reaches 4,000. Then, too, huge flat-topped hills rise abruptly from this great plateau, and irregular valleys cut it up in almost any direction. You can see, from this, that the country offers problems to the flier.

But in addition to the elevation of the country over which we were to fly, we immediately ran head-on into fog, just as we reached the first great terrace of hills and mountains within half an hour of the time we left Cape Town.

Now flying in the fog over a range of strange mountains leaves much to be desired, and as the "ceiling" grew lower and lower, with the mountains ahead of us growing higher at the same time, Boris, quite properly, began to look for a way out. We were so overloaded with supplies and equipment that we carried gasoline for only seven hours, while Carstens, in the smaller plane, carried enough only for five.

Time after time Boris tried to get through, only to have the fog close down. The other plane would fade from sight in the shredded fog, and Boris would be forced to bank and turn and break once more into the clear air from which we had come. Back and forth along the edge of that cloud bank we flew, trying here and there to make our way through it but not until we had searched for thirty miles along its front was Boris able to find a way, and only then by flying low through a pass.

But hardly had we time to congratulate ourselves when the fog closed down. We could see nothing but the gray murk. Vern and his plane disappeared utterly, and I don't hesitate to admit that Osa and I were frightened. We had all the confidence in the world in Boris, and never for a moment were we frightened for ourselves. But our shiny new planes, that had looked so bright and perfect on the flying field only a little while before—how awful if they should be wrecked.

For half an hour we were utterly and hopelessly lost in that fog, wondering all that time what might happen next —wondering, too, what on earth had happened to Vern and the other plane. And then, quite suddenly, a beautiful valley appeared below us, and there behind us came Vern, as if following the leader through such a pea-soup fog were the simplest thing in all the world.

But though the fog had cleared away below us, it hung heavily above, and suddenly we lost Vern. By now, too, we had been in the air almost five hours, and though our plane still had a reserve of gasoline, we knew that Vern's supply must be running low. It was all very discouraging, but on we went, dodging the low-hanging clouds as best we could until, finally, we sighted the flying field at the little town of Victoria West, and landed to find a telephone message from Vern. He had been forced to land a hundred miles or so back, at the town of Beauford West in order to take on gas, and before we had finished lunch at the town hotel Vern came in. We had made about 350 miles, in spite of the fog, and it was with some relief that we learned from the weather reports that the sky was clear ahead of us.

Over African Jungles

Even then we flew only as far as Kimberley, another 250 miles, before calling it a day.

The next morning we made the 300-mile hop to Pretoria before ten o'clock, but had to stop there for repairs. Our oil was heating so badly that we spent three days installing oil coolers, before taking off for Pietersburg and Bulawayo. We lost Vern again that day, for his plane was slower than ours, and somewhere in the vicinity of the Limpopo River —the one that Kipling calls "the great, green, greasy Limpopo River"—he dropped behind. We landed at Bulawayo and shortly Vern arrived, but when we took off for Salisbury we lost him again. We landed at the flying field just at dusk, and proceeded to wait for Vern. It grew darker and darker, and still no word from Vern. Kerosene flares were set out, but there were only six of them and they did not serve to light up much of that section of Rhodesia. Osa and I wondered how Vern could ever find the field at all. More time passed, and it grew darker still, with only those six flickering lights to mark the flying field, and then we heard his motor. We couldn't see the plane, though presently we could make out its lights. He flew low over the field several times, but it did not seem possible for a pilot to land in that unlighted place. Yet down he came and rolled up to the hangar as if landing on strange, unlighted African flying fields was another very simple task.

But by now we were a good 1,600 miles from Cape Town, and had reached the last of the settled country. We had been flying over beautiful farming country, but now

11

we were definitely headed for the wilds, with the Zambezi River just ahead. We were beginning to feel that we had at last reached the Africa that we knew, and Osa got out her fishing tackle, and suggested that we land on the river. We even stocked up with provisions against the possibility of spending several days there.

Without our suspecting it, the weather man had plans of his own. Furthermore, within an hour of Salisbury, we found the mountains; and they are mountains, too, I can assure you—great, rugged, rocky crags, with narrow, twisting valleys that are, in many places, no more than canyons. There wasn't the faintest sign of any habitation, and a more impossible country in which to land an airplane would be hard to find. And then, quite unexpectedly, we saw the Zambezi River—nowhere near where the map showed it to be. And as if that were not enough, the clouds closed in. Time after time we tried to find our way over the mountains, but the clouds grew more and more dense and presently it began to rain.

For an hour we flew up and down the river, trying vainly to find some landmark that we could recognize, but it was hopeless. We were lost—no doubt about it—but in addition to that, we had lost Vern and the other plane. We had taken off with gas enough for only five hours and time was passing. The weather was getting worse, as well. Boris kept studying the map that I held in front of him, and I tried to study it, too, though I could make out nothing whatever that meant a thing to me.

Over African Jungles

And then, quite suddenly and for no reason that I could see, Boris turned and headed away from the river. What he had seen or guessed or figured out I don't know to this day, but I would trust him anywhere, and neither Osa nor I said a word. Anyway, we had already seen that he could not land on the river. It was far narrower than we had expected it to be, and in addition was the crookedest stream that one could imagine. There apparently was nothing to do except hunt for an emergency landing field somewhere else.

We had been in the air for more than four hours—less than an hour's supply of gasoline left, and quite suddenly we saw a railroad. That, at least, was on our map. We could smile, now, and we did. We passed over a little station and tried to see its sign, but we failed. On we flew. Another station, but still no sign. But now the sky began to clear. That, certainly, was in our favor, but a glance at our gasoline gauge gave us something else to worry over. It stood at zero, and still no possible landing field in sight. Visibility was perfect, now, but there was no sign of the town of Broken Hill which, we knew, had a flying field. Every moment we expected the motors to stutter and quit, yet on we flew. The country below us was wooded and rough, and we could visualize ourselves crashing in the trees at almost any moment. Only Boris was cheerful, and managed somehow to talk and laugh in an effort to keep our minds off that gasoline gauge.

And then Broken Hill appeared. In another moment Boris

13

had set the big ship down in a perfect three-point landing, and there were Vern and the others ahead of us. We had no sooner landed than Boris set about testing the gas tanks. He laughed when he had sounded their depths.

"Why," he remarked, "we still have enough for another ten minutes."

One might imagine that such an experience would have taken some of the enthusiasm out of us, but bright and early the next morning we were at the field again, as eager as ever to get into the air, with the sky clear and Mpeka, so we were told, only three hours away.

It is not unlikely, however, that Mr. Sikorsky and the American Department of Commerce, Aviation Division, would have failed to approve our load. In the big ship, besides the five of us, were a dozen well-filled suit cases, a dozen boxes of supplies, aerial cameras, emergency food, a couple of rifles, plenty of reading matter, and in addition to still other belongings a sixth passenger in the form of Wah, our pet gibbon ape from Borneo. Wah was the most enthusiastic flyer of us all. He loved to look out the windows and watch the landscape glide past. He never worried about getting lost, and trifles such as empty gasoline tanks troubled him not at all. He divided his time between looking out the windows, begging for food, going from one of us to another in order to be petted, and perching on the steering wheel as Boris piloted the ship. And on taking off from Broken Hill the rest of us were as happy as Wah.

Everything went perfectly. We had five hours' supply

of gasoline for a three-hour hop, and the weather was perfect. We found the hills and roads that were marked on the map, and trouble seemed very far away indeed.

We followed the line of a road we could see beneath us, expecting to land at Mpeka within three hours, but shortly we became conscious of the fact that the road and the map did not agree. Three hours passed and Mpeka did not appear. Four hours. Still no Mpeka. Vern had dropped out of sight astern long before, for the big plane was the faster, but when, after four hours, our destination failed to appear, we began to wonder where we were. We turned back in an attempt to find some landmark or other. No luck. The country below us was now a mass of mountains, deep canyons, and little streams. Here and there some native village appeared, but not a thing could we see that we could locate on the map, and there was not an acre of open space on which to land.

The gasoline gauge sank to zero, and once again we listened tensely for the spluttering of the motors that would tell us that the flight was about to end. Of course, we knew from our experience of the day before that zero on that gauge was, in reality, a little above zero—that a *little* gas was left. But I can assure you that it is neither humorous nor pleasantly exciting to sit in such a plane and watch, with one eye, a gauge that marks an empty gas tank, and with the other to look out the windows, down onto seemingly endless mountains and gorges, rocks and trees and

15

cliffs, among which a safe landing could not possibly be made.

Minute after minute passed, and with each revolution of our roaring motors we knew that our pitifully meager supply of gas was disappearing. On the day before we had flown for eight or nine minutes, perhaps, after the gauge stood at zero, and then had landed with a little gas in the tanks—with enough, so Boris had said, for ten minutes more in the air. But now as the minutes passed, I wondered if we really *had* flown for eight or nine minutes beyond the "zero mark," or had our imaginations only made it seem so. And had Boris really measured accurately, and had there been ten full minutes' supply left when we had landed? If those two assumptions had been true, then we could keep going for eighteen or nineteen minutes. If they were not, there was no telling when the motors would falter and stop, leaving us to crash among those abrupt and twisting valleys and canyons, or on one of those steep and rocky mountainsides, or in among the trees that clustered here and there.

Five minutes passed, and still the motors roared sturdily on, while Wah, quite unworried by the danger that stared us in the face, climbed down from his perch on the steering wheel to curl up in my lap. I paid no attention to him, but he chattered gently, begging to be petted. I stroked him once or twice, glanced at the gasoline gauge again, and stared through the window at the endless ruggedness below us.

Ten minutes passed, and even Boris found it harder to

SAFARI TENT. Osa under the veranda of our safari tent. These tents consist of one regular tent with a fly overall, about ten inches above the tent proper, which allowed circulation of cool air between. In the rear is a bath addition. This is a flashlight photograph made just at sundown. In the box can be seen Wah ready to go to sleep for the night.

DINING TENT. Interior. In the foreground are canvas water coolers. Evaporation causes the water inside to cool from five to eight degrees below the temperature of the air. Our tinned provisions consist of all the luxuries of Europe and America.

SIMBA. The King of Beasts is afraid of nothing and seldom harms human beings unless he is provoked, or thinks he is cornered. He is always fat, sleek, and contented. The Serengetti Plains in Tanganyika ... tive than any other part of Africa.

keep up his flow of humorous and entertaining comment. Wah was with Osa by now, and she was quietly stroking him, saying nothing, and thinking I don't know what. We were all growing more nervous by the minute, but, oddly enough, were growing quieter as well. There were no hysterics—no expressed fear—no heroics. We just sat, saying a little now and then, but nervously watching the motionless gasoline gauge and staring out the windows.

Fifteen minutes passed. It is extraordinary how long that quarter of an hour had been, yet, though the time that had passed seemed an age and we were flying at about one hundred miles an hour, we seemed to be floating along through the air as slowly and aimlessly as does the down from a dandelion. The mountains and canyons and valleys slid so slowly below us as to remind me of a slow-motion picture, and though they were always changing—slowly—they gave me the strange idea that they really were always the same, and were merely changing their shape, as one sees the waves of the ocean do on a stormy day.

I had assumed that nineteen minutes would positively see the end of our gasoline supply, and I tensely watched the clock on the instrument board as the hand approached the nineteenth minute. Closer and closer it crept, and still the motors roared. The nineteenth minute came and went. The twentieth minute came. For a minute and a half I believe my eyes never left that slowly moving minute hand. But I could watch it no longer. I glanced up and out the window. For a moment the bright light outside prevented my seeing

17

clearly, but as I blinked my eyes I thought I saw the reflec-
tion of light in the distance. I blinked them again and
looked. There was something, certainly. I reached for my
binoculars and looked, and managed, somehow, to speak to
Boris quite calmly.

"There's a lake over there, Boris," I remarked.

He glanced quickly in the direction in which I was pointing, and nodding casually changed the course of the ship
toward the lake which appeared fairly clearly now.

It was, I suppose, six or seven miles away when I first
saw it—four minutes of flying, perhaps. But did we have
gas for four minutes? Three minutes' supply might do, perhaps, for we could glide for some distance. Possibly even
two minutes' supply might serve. But already we had flown
for nearly twenty-one minutes on a supply that only my
greatest optimism had permitted me to estimate as being
enough for nineteen minutes. Yet the motors had not fal-
tered even for a moment. The twenty-first minute passed.
Twenty-one and a half! How slowly we seemed to move!
Twenty-two! The lake was not far off by now and seemed
to be all of two miles wide, by three or perhaps four in
length.

I'm sure I held my breath. It was only a matter of seconds
that would tell us whether we would reach the water and
land safely, or whether the motors would stop and we would
crash on the very edge of safety.

Certainly, by now, the gasoline *must* be consumed. Yet on
we went, and finally after the longest minutes I have ever

lived, we were actually over the water. How beautiful that lake seemed to be. What lake it was we did not know. We could not find it on our map. It was, no doubt, scores—perhaps a hundred—miles from any gasoline supply, but that made little difference. We could land safely—that was certain, at last—and if necessary we could camp on the shore for days or weeks while we sent for gasoline.

Boris brought the plane down onto the smooth water, and then we caught sight of a cluster of buildings at the upper end of the lake. We taxied toward them, and as the plane slid her nose into the reeds that marked the shore line, we saw scores and scores of natives running toward us, and following them, a white man and a white woman.

I must admit that the first thing that came to my mind was Rider Haggard's story "Alan Quatermain." Of course, in Haggard's story the hero and his companions had reached their Central African lake by means of an underground river, while we had arrived at ours by air. And they, of course, found a whole nation of white people, with a beautiful capital city built of marble, while we had found only one white man and his wife, though their home, it later developed, would have done justice to Haggard's imagination. As a matter of fact what we found seemed almost as strange as anything in fiction.

The lady and gentleman who greeted us were Lieutenant-Colonel and Mrs. Stewart Gore-Browne who, when the colonel had retired from the British Army, had come to this far-distant corner of Africa, and had built themselves a mansion that would have been unusual even in Buckingham-shire or Westchester. It was, in reality, almost a castle, on which they had already spent five years in the building, and were still expecting to spend two more before they could complete it. It stands a hundred miles or so from any town whatever, contains thirty-five rooms, and is as lovely a place as one could hope to find.

They had, of course, heard our motors before we landed, and not realizing that our plane was an amphibian, they had imagined that we would all be drowned when they saw us descend upon the lake.

What wonderful people the colonel and his wife imme-diately proved to be! We were invited to lunch the moment we stepped ashore, and when we commented on the fact that we had landed with almost our last drop of petrol (the tank was actually dry and only a little remained in the feed pipes) the colonel hastened to tell us that he could supply us with enough to take the plane back to Mpeka—which we had missed and overflown. He explained that on another occasion a plane had been forced down in one of his pas-tures, and the aviator had had to wait a week for a mes-senger to go out and for gasoline to be sent in. It was then that the colonel had decided to lay in a supply of aviation petrol in case such a thing happened again. After lunch, therefore, while Osa and I remained with Colonel Gore-Browne and his wife, Boris took off with the borrowed petrol, and flew to Mpeka, where he found Carstens won-dering what had happened to us. Having filled their tanks

RENDILLE WOMEN. Every day the Rendille women came to our Ngroon camp to inspect our birds. They were interested in the fact that we flew like birds, but they never showed any curiosity about the mechanics of it. It was just another marvelous thing the white man did. They let it go at that.

STAMPEDE. A herd of giraffe startled by our big airplanes ran awkwardly in circles. As a rule the game paid very little attention to our planes but the giraffe, because of their greater height, could possibly see us better and they always stampeded at our approach. We were afraid they might step into a big hole or injure themselves so we rarely bothered them.

the two planes returned and landed on a field that the colonel had prepared for such emergencies.

We spent the night at this most romantic and hospitable place, and took off the following morning for Mbeya, in Tanganyika Territory, with the firm intention, which we still hold, of returning some day to revisit these delightful people in their extraordinary home.

From the time we had left Cape Town we had been flying over territory new to us. We have spent years in Africa, but our interest has been in the animals of that continent, with the result that we have confined ourselves to those regions where animals can most readily be found. And on the day we took off from the home that Colonel and Mrs. Gore-Browne had built there on their distant lake, we landed in Tanganyika Territory, and felt, once more, that we were on familiar ground. Many times we had visited Tanganyika. Our motor cars had often taken us from Nairobi to the lion country of that region, and I had exposed thousands of feet of film all about the Tanganyika plains. Now we were to fly over them, with Nairobi, and the only home we have ever owned, only a short flight beyond.

We reached Mbeya before noon, a bit worried for Vern, for we had seen him down in a field beside a native village. It is true that he had signaled that everything was all right, but it wasn't until he had caught up with us that we learned that he had landed in order to ask his directions. Fortunately, too, he had found a native who could speak enough English to direct him.

Just before dusk we reached Dodoma, but found, to our dismay, that the flying field was a veritable lake. The light was poor, too, and we could not tell clearly just how deep the water was. Here and there about its smooth expanse black spots stood clear of the water, but whether they were rocks or mud we could not guess. Back and forth over the field we flew, wondering whether to try a landing on our wheels or on our boat-shaped hull. It was all very discouraging, but finally Boris made up his mind, lowered the wheels, and tried it. Down we came, there was a gentle jolt, and immediately the mud and water flew wide in blinding sheets. Instantly our plane was literally plastered with mud. The windows were spattered with it. The wings were smeared, and the tail was dripping. We skidded sickeningly, and great sheets of muddy water flew past. But finally we slid to a halt, and Vern followed our muddy example, with no harm whatever except to the immaculate appearance of our planes.

And now, in reality, we were close to home. We found a dry section of the field the following morning, and took off at sunrise. Almost at once we sighted a herd of buffalo, and I watched eagerly to see what effect a plane would have on them. They are noble beasts, these African buffalo, and afraid of nothing—nothing, that is, that they understand. But what could such a herd do against so giant a bird as our plane must have seemed to be—a bird, too, that made a noise equal to half a dozen roaring lions, and that was colored in the manner of a zebra? They tried to hold their ground, and yet, against so extraordinary a creature as this, that had so suddenly and noisily appeared above them, they dared not. They stamped the earth. They hesitated. They turned and ran, and in a moment they stampeded. But in that moment we had passed them and were roaring off into the distance. I turned to watch them, and saw them slow down. And now they stopped and looked around, and stamped their feet once more, and wondered, no doubt, just what it was that had come and gone so noisily and so quickly.

I have seen the same thing many times since, as I saw it that morning for the first time. And on that morning I saw herds of other animals do much the same thing. Kongoni— zebra—giraffe. And what, I wonder, could those zebra and giraffe have thought at seeing two huge and noisy birds so gaudily dressed in costumes like their own?

But now there was almost too much to watch, for every valley and every hill and mountain were old friends of ours. There lay the plains where live the friendly lions that we had photographed. Far off to the east loomed the vast and snow-capped shape of beautiful Kilimanjaro. Almost beside us glided Mt. Longido, and there ahead lay the Athi Plains, once the marvel of the animal world. Then we caught the glitter of the sun on the rails of the line from Mombasa to Nairobi. How many times we had ridden up and down the line since first we had come to Africa twelve short years before.

Over African Jungles

And now Nairobi appeared upon the plain—we flew over the town, and pointed out its familiar landmarks to our companions. We circled the flying field, and Boris put the big ship down. She rolled and bumped to a stop, the motors idling, and suddenly we were surrounded by a cheering, laughing throng—friends, acquaintances, strangers—all eager to welcome us back—back home. The American consul welcomed us, and motor cars came tearing out from town, having seen us as we passed.

We climbed happily from the plane, and made our way to our home in Muthalga on the outskirts of Nairobi. How good it looked, with all our old "boys" who, years before, had carried our belongings on those long, slow, foot safaris, and some of whom, now, were the gardeners and handymen and pensioners at this home of ours in Africa.

Here we were once more, ready to begin the greatest of all our safaris—the most romantic, the very happiest of all our many expeditions into the blue. What more could any person want?—friends, home, and the work that seems to us the very happiest in the world. And now we had two gorgeous, able planes, as well, to take us farther into the field than we had ever gone before. It almost seemed as if the magic carpet now were ours, to use as we saw fit about this magic world of Africa.

LANDING SUPPLIES FROM NAIROBI. Vern has just landed with a fresh supply of film and provisions from Nairobi. Such scenes as this make me wonder how we ever got along without airplanes on previous safaris.

CHARGE OF A RHINO. Osa and I were inside our small plane when this picture was made. The rhino came charging out of the bush and we feared, for a few seconds, that he was going to break up our plane. But, on coming within ten feet, he must have decided that he'd never seen such a huge bird before. He stopped, thought it over, and then turned tail and ran on.

2

IT WAS two months after we arrived in Nairobi before we were ready to go into the field. There were literally hundreds of things to be attended to before we could start—a hangar to build at the Nairobi landing field; cameras to clean, to repair, to adjust, and to test; the same for lenses; and an almost infinite variety of tasks revolved about our sound equipment. Then, too, we had to organize our plans and our supplies before we could go winging off into the outlying country, for airplanes use gasoline, even in Africa, though there are few places in those portions of the continent that we planned to visit where it can be obtained. Thus it was up to us to see that it was sent ahead, and just as Roy Chapman Andrews often sent spare tires and extra gasoline and oil into the Gobi Desert by camel train, in order that his motor cars might have what they required, so we used all sorts of means of transportation in order, first, to make certain that landing fields would be available where Nature had not had the foresight to prepare them, and, second, that gasoline and oil and other supplies would be on hand in these same regions.

Within a week of the time of our arrival in Nairobi both Boris Sergievsky and Al Morway returned to the United

States, for they had come only in order to help us get our planes to Nairobi. The rest of us, however, worked early and late at the endless tasks, big and little, that were so absolutely essential to the success of whatever we attempted in the field.

Years before, Osa and I had discovered a spot far to the north of Nairobi that we had ever since planned to revisit, and it was with that spot in mind that we were preparing.

If you care to look at a map of British East Africa—officially it is Kenya Colony now—you will find that a long and comparatively narrow lake—Lake Rudolf—extends south from the border of Abyssinia for 175 miles or so, and that a valley, edged by the rugged and difficult Mathews Range and the equally difficult Ndoto Mountains, runs on south of Lake Rudolf for many miles more. This valley varies greatly in width, being ten or fifteen miles across in some places. It is broken into by countless side valleys, is interrupted by hills and mountains of its own, and in one place, about midway of its length, narrows down between the towering mountains that enclose it until it is hardly more than a good two hundred yards in width. This spot is roughly seventy or eighty miles south of Lake Rudolf, and it was the place we particularly had in mind.

It must be remembered that this portion of Africa does not have seasons as we know them. Instead of winter and summer, spring and fall, the native of Kenya Colony has only the dry season and "the rains." The movements of game, too, are powerfully influenced by this fact, and as we were interested in the game, we were forced to plan accordingly.

Now on our previous visit to this narrow point in the great valley, we had seen an infinite number of signs that had told us very plainly that the valley as a whole is a sort of migration route for countless elephants, and we had figured out that though they might spread out and wander into almost any side valley, and even reach the higher country to the north and south of that narrow place, most of them—or at least a very large proportion of them—would, in the natural course of their migrations, pass between those high and rocky walls that narrowed the valley so greatly at that particular point. And what, we thought, would be better than to be there when it happened, and to photograph, if our luck was good, a veritable sea of elephants flowing through that narrow pass at the high tide of their migration?

So far so good. But the trouble was that these migrations take place during "the rains," and I can assure you that travel leaves something to be desired in Africa at that time of the year when one is far from roads and trails, as this spot is. It remained for us, then, to get there before the rains, erect a permanent camp, prepare a flying field that would not become a quagmire when the rains arrived, and otherwise prepare to photograph those countless elephants that we were so intent on observing.

By the same token, we dared not camp at that exact spot,

for fear of disrupting the natural movements of the elephants. Consequently, we chose a spot of which we knew, called Ngronet, and situated about ten miles to the north of the pass, and within sixty or seventy miles of Lake Rudolf.

I do not, however, wish to give anyone the impression that because this spot has a name it has anything else, for it really does not. It has a name because of the fact that in a region that becomes as parched and dry as dust in the dry season, it has a little collection of springs which always, no matter how delayed the rains may be, manage to continue to give forth their small flow of water.

These springs, then, would serve a double purpose. They would supply our camp with water, and at the same time would serve to attract the animals of the vicinity before the arrival of the rains and the time for the elephant migration that was our major interest. Furthermore, camping at such a distance from the pass we could reach it without too much difficulty and without running the risk of interfering with the normal movements of the migrating animals.

All of these plans were carefully prepared in Nairobi, but because a landing field at Ngronet was something that Mother Nature had neglected to install, we had to send a party ahead in order to have one prepared. And, too, though the distance is only about 400 miles, it is 400 miles largely devoid of roads and for a considerable part of the way devoid even of trails. Consequently, though we later several times made the trip by air in three and a half hours, we decided to give the automobile party two weeks in which to get there, and an extra week in which to grub up the shrubs and remove the irregularities from what was to be our private flying field in these highly uncivilized parts. We arranged, too, to have a "wind sock" erected to aid us in our landing, and to have certain signals set out on this field to tell us, when we arrived overhead, whether or not it was ready to receive us, or, if not, when it would be.

We had been very careful indeed to plan thoughtfully, and the result was that when, almost exactly two months after we had reached Nairobi from Cape Town, we arose at the crack of dawn, boarded our big, two-motored plane at the flying field, and took off for Ngronet, everything went perfectly. Osa and I knew the country over which we were flying—our maps were good—the early morning air was perfect for flying—and three hours and twenty minutes later we were circling our new flying field on which we could make out the big white cross that told us we could land. Down we came, in one of Vern's perfect three-point landings, and we were, at last, about to begin the work that had taken us to Africa.

From long experience we have learned how to set up a perfect camp, and we went about it at once. The motor party had brought quantities of material. We had brought more in the plane, and within a few days Osa, Vern Carstens, Sanial, Moreno, Davis and I, with our thirteen "boys" from Nairobi, were as comfortable as one could ask. The principal difficulty lay in the fact that the water holes were several miles away, up a winding, twisting, rocky way, and that, owing to an excessively dry season, every other water hole for scores of miles around had dried up. This might have been to our advantage, had it not been for the fact that the Samburu and Rendille natives of the region, with thousands of head of camels, sheep, and goats were constantly visiting these same water holes. All day long the slowly moving line came up the valley, and all day long another slowly moving line of watered stock moved down again, turning off here and there in search of the scant pasturage that still remained before returning once more for water. Each herdsman visited the water hole on every third day, but so numerous were they, and so numerous their flocks, that hardly an hour of any day passed without adding to the numbers of that endless, bleating, complaining line of forever-moving herds.

Nevertheless, we had planned long and carefully, and were not to be driven off by any silly difficulty such as that. We inveigled a couple of Rendille tribesmen to put seven of their camels to work carrying water for our camp, and knowing that the herdsmen would leave the water hole severely alone at night, in order the better to protect their herds from the lions and the leopards, we realized that during the dark hours we might be able to use the place for our own purposes. It then became obvious that we were fortunate, for if the natives had to bring their stock from miles around to this particular spot, the animals from at least as large an area were forced to use it as well. Furthermore, they were kept away from the water all day long by the never-failing line of herdsmen and herds, and so came in even greater numbers at night.

Even before we had finished the work of setting up camp to our satisfaction we learned that we were in an almost ideal spot. Animals were not only plentiful, they were of every local species as well. As always, the antelope were most plentiful. We were forever seeing a few greater and many lesser kudu, as they browsed upon the leaves on the difficult surrounding mountainsides, or stood staring at us from a distance, their graceful heads up, and the beautiful spirals of their horns silhouetted against the rocks. Chapman's zebras were common, and their barking—they do not bray, despite their relationship to the lowly ass—was forever to be heard. Grevy's zebras, too, were always about—much larger and handsomer than their commoner cousins, and capable of braying with all the fervency of any Missouri mule. Giraffe appeared now and then in the distance, their odd heads motionless as they gazed across the stunted trees, or their legs defying all the laws of mechanics as they ran at our approach. Elephants appeared in groups now and then. Buffalo appeared in herds of thirty or forty at almost any time, and rhinos—well, if anything, the ugly, cantankerous beasts were a bit too numerous, sometimes, for comfort.

There were not many lions about, but a night never passed without their air-quivering roars, and now and then we saw them during the day, while leopards were really numerous, and hyenas, jackals, wart hogs and the smaller animals were everywhere.

The water hole, being well up in the rocky hills, did not offer a very good camp site, but three miles or so down the twisting valley lay a circular and more or less level spot a mile or two in diameter, where, at some distance from the trail by which the native herdsmen drove their endless herds, we pitched our tents. To the north of us the hills and mountains rose abruptly. To the south, across the parched expanse of this amphitheater, the hills rose again, the valley narrowed, twisted, and descended until, some seven miles from camp, it opened out onto a really level stretch upon which our flying field had been built. It was forever necessary, consequently, for us to be going back and forth from flying field to camp, from camp to water hole, as well as on prospecting trips for animals in other directions.

The result of this was that we soon began to see the possibilities that lay about us, although if we had been so inexcusably unobservant as not to see them, we would have had them called to our attention by Boculy, who had been with us on every expedition we have made to Africa, and was the most extraordinarily capable elephant tracker I have ever seen—one of the very best, I am inclined to believe, who ever lived. Elephants were Boculy's specialty, and a specialist he was, but he was remarkably capable when it came to animals of any other sort, as well, and was a walking encyclopedia on all related subjects. As a matter of fact, he was all against our "wasting" so much time pre-

CONGO ELEPHANT. A fine young female elephant who was so curious that she walked towards us and backed away several times before deciding to leave. This picture was made in the Ituri Forest in the Belgian Congo. Her tusks are very thin as are the tusks of all the Congo elephants. Seldom do female tusks weigh more than 35 pounds in this part of Africa.

THE ENTIRE WORLD. This small island in the southern end of Lake Rudolf was supposed to be uninhabited until a British expedition visited them about two years before I made this picture from my plane. The story is that these savages thought they were the entire population of the world up to that time. They are only 87 by actual count and their home is the most desolate place on earth. They live almost entirely on fish.

paring our flying field, and almost hourly during every day he came in with most urgent news (as he saw it), insisting that we drop our work for the opportunity to photograph this or that or something else.

We, however, were almost momentarily expecting the rains, and we knew that if they descended too soon, our flying field would become so muddy that we could not take off. And there were other tasks beside. Davis was busy setting cameras along the trails, in order that passing animals might photograph themselves by touching a wire. Sanial was constantly working with the sound equipment, and was busily engaged in instructing Moreno in its use, for Moreno was to take charge of it when Sanial returned to "the States." Consequently we kept putting Boculy off until, at last, he began to show signs of losing interest in what, after all, was his job, and a most important one—the job of being forever on the alert for the animals that we had to photograph. Consequently I permitted him to lead me off to photograph something, and having started, in that way, on the work we were there to perform, I left the flying field more and more to Vern, and set about the task of studying the animals and photographing them. Vern made flights, now and then, to Nairobi or Archer's Post or Lasimis water hole (where we had cached some supplies) to bring up this and that. The boys smoothed the trail a bit between camp and the flying field. Our two Rendille natives and their seven camels made two round trips daily from camp to the water hole for water, while Osa, Sanial, Moreno, Davis and

I set about our business of animal photography (with, as we say in the movies, natural sound).

It was, as I recall it, about this time that Vern Carstens flew down to our cache at Lasimis water hole one afternoon, planning to load the plane and spend the night, returning the following day. He did exactly as he had planned, returning to Ngronet an hour or so after we had had breakfast. But instead of recording a casual and uneventful trip, he brought back a story that I feel certain he must be telling yet.

He had, so he told us, arrived early enough to get the supplies for which he had gone into the plane before dusk, after which he had prepared his supper, and being tired and alone, decided to turn in early. The sky was perfectly clear, and he set up his cot on the sand beneath one of the plane's wings, unrolled his blankets, and climbed in. The animal sounds he heard were unexciting, and because he had parked the plane three or four miles across the sand from the water hole itself, he assumed that the animals would not be likely to approach it.

With this comforting thought in mind, consequently, he had promptly gone to sleep, and, as luck would have it, was untroubled for several hours. In that time, however, the full moon reached a point fairly well overhead, lighting up the sandy surroundings of the water hole with a counterfeit daylight of extraordinary brightness. This part of his description tallies with my own observations at the same place, where Osa and I have often camped. I know of no place where the moonlight seems brighter.

But now, to go on with Vern's story, he was awakened by a sound which seemed, at the moment, to be the explosive hiss of exhaust steam escaping through the stack of a locomotive. Locomotives, however, have never been known to visit the moonlit sands of Lasimis water hole, as Vern realized the instant he awoke. But at the moment it is probable that his sleep-befuddled brain did not interpret the sound further. Instead, he sat up abruptly and stared out across the sands where every object stood out almost with daylight clarity. And there, far too close for comfort—perhaps thirty or forty yards away—a big rhino was as apparent to Vern as any haystack might have been. Furthermore, to make the matter perfectly clear, the rhino, at the sound Vern made in sitting up, let out his explosive snort once more and came forward a few steps before stopping and snorting a third time.

Now Osa and I have had many experiences with rhinos. We have met scores—hundreds—of the ugly-tempered fellows all about British East and elsewhere. They have trotted about us and snorted at us and threatened us for years, and we know what possibilities of serious danger reside in their powerful, wrinkled bodies, and in their saber-curved horns. Yet we have always met them when we were armed and were consequently more or less able to defend ourslves.

Yet here was Vern—alone in a camp cot, and with a snorting rhino apparently bent on making trouble. Furthermore, it was the first rhino Vern had met, and his rifle, unfortunately, was in the plane. To make a bad matter worse, too, a second and only slightly smaller rhino appeared in the moonlight not far behind the first.

Now it is likely that Vern did not realize one piece of good fortune that was his. He had, as I have said, placed his cot beneath one of the plane's wings, and as a result he was somewhat obscured by the shadow of it. A rhino's eyes are not the best in the world, and it seems to me likely that with the moonlight bright all about, the snorting old fellow failed to see Vern, and saw, instead, the much more bulky shape of the plane. Still, Vern's scent, and the other scents that emanated from the plane, were anathema to the rhino and his mate, though the motionless plane, with Vern invisible, or nearly so, in the shadow, might have seemed, even to a rhino, as something too big to tackle.

However, Vern was no expert in rhino psychology, and I can imagine that even had he thought of the protection the shadow was giving him, he might have felt—and quite properly—that shadows are, at best, unsubstantial things with which to oppose a couple of tons of cantankerous rhino, armed, on his ugly nose, with a two-foot horn quite capable of ripping holes even through the fuselage of the plane.

So there sat Vern, protected by his two blankets and the shadow, while the rhino snorted and trotted forward, paused and stamped his feet, backed up a few steps, and trotted in circles, snorting the while. The second rhino seemed to act, so Vern said, more or less as a rear guard or a reserve force.

SUNNING CROCODILES. Movie enlargement. Crocodiles sunning themselves on the banks of the Victoria Nile. This is an everyday sight along the crocodile-infested African rivers. Enormous fellows lie close together for miles up and down a stream where fish are to be found in the deep pools. The sounder a crocodile sleeps, the more his mouth opens; birds often walk in and pick food from between his teeth. If he is awakened suddenly, his jaws fly shut with the report of a small rifle.

UNINHABITED, BLEAK, AND HOT. The kind of country that makes an aviator's hair turn gray. Hundreds of miles of this sort of barren country along the shores of Lake Rudolf, uninhabited, bleak, and hot. Mostly volcanic lava covered with sand.

It snorted and trotted and stamped in much the same manner as the first, but at a somewhat greater distance, as if
awaiting the outcome of whatever the first one might decide
to do before taking a more important part.

And still Vern sat in the camp cot wondering what to do,
though by now he had carefully freed his feet so that he
could leap out with no fear of being tangled in the blankets.
He thought constantly of his rifle, but to get it he would
have to leap from his cot, scurry twenty feet toward the tail
of the fuselage, which would have brought him somewhat
closer to the rhino, and there he would have had to scramble
onto the fuselage, slide the hatch open and get inside.

It didn't look like a good plan, for the rhino might
charge, and even though Vern might have escaped—might
even have got the gun and fired it—it was far too possible
that that vicious horn might by that time tear through the
thin sides of the fuselage, or that the blundering beast might
get tangled up among the struts and supports of the tail.

Now all of this, I contend, points clearly to the fact that
Vern's position was not a pleasant one. There was literally
nothing to be done, so that is exactly what Vern did. That
is, he did nothing but watch those snorting, trotting, paw-
ing beasts for a full three quarters of an hour, during which
they were at no time more than sixty or seventy yards from
him and often must have seemed almost close enough for
him to feel the wind from their prodigious snorts.

But finally, as is the way of rhinos, they gave up being
incensed at Vern's presence and withdrew while Vern, I sus-

pect, drew a sigh of relief and wished them a long, long journey. But he had had what sleep he got that night. Anyway, dawn was only another hour or so away, and the light was no stronger than necessary when he took off.

That was the reason he arrived at Ngronet within an hour of the time we had had our breakfast. And it was then that he got his, for he had neglected the matter at Lasimis water hole.

Nor do I mean to be facetious about his adventure. He was in no position to defend himself, and though he might have thrown his cot at the rhino if it had charged, he could have done little more except dodge. And I have always appreciated the fact that he thought of what that rhino might do to the plane. For, you see, it was *my* plane.

It is difficult to recall now, even with the aid of my notes, the exact sequence of events at Ngronet. But Vern's experience with the rhinos reminds me of Hugh Davis's first intimate experience with elephants. The principal difference between the two stories lies in the fact that Hugh has so great a sense of humor that even in recounting what must have been a real adventure he could not resist adding a touch or two of the ridiculous.

He was forever searching along the game trails in the vicinity for likely places to set up his "still" cameras, from which he led wires so that animals, in passing, would trip the shutters and record themselves on the negatives. On one day in particular he was in a narrow little gorge-like valley with walls almost too steep to climb, and as he rounded a rock, he ran squarely into a herd of seven elephants. The exact details of what happened have never been clear to me, for Hugh, in recounting the adventure, has always made so much of a joke of the matter that my mind is not clear on the salient facts. It seems plain, however, that he very properly beat a hasty retreat, only to find in a very few seconds, that three *other* elephants were coming toward him from the other direction. But here again, because of Hugh's sense of the ridiculous, I am hazy as to the details. I only know that Hugh appeared in camp very much out of breath, but with his cameras and equipment.

"I don't know," he explained, somewhat breathlessly, "who was scared the most—the elephants or me. But I know I ran the fastest."

Ngronet was our base camp for two months and a half, which was something we had not planned. We had hurried to reach the place ahead of the rains, and had worked early and late to prepare both camp and landing field so that they would be usable while the rains were at their worst. And, much to our surprise and disappointment, the rains never materialized. Thus, the great elephant migration upon which we had based all our plans failed to materialize as well, and we were forced to rearrange our plans and look for other worlds to conquer.

During all our stay at Ngronet we were forever seeing both Samburu and Rendille natives. Now and then, too, Turkanas appeared at camp. But we saw little of especial interest in these tribes—perhaps because we knew them too well—and tried from time to time to plan some way in which we could inveigle some of the Ndorobos of the mountains to lay aside their wildness for a time, in order that we might photograph them.

These Ndorobos are a queer people, and it is not impossible that some of my information concerning them is less than absolutely accurate. But, subject to that reservation, their story is more or less as follows.

They are, to begin with, to be found in the wilder and less accessible regions throughout British East, and the more trustworthy natives—whether Samburu, Rendille, Masai, Lumbwa, Turkana or whatnot—have nothing whatever to do with them—seem, on the contrary, to fear them. Yet, when one begins to ask questions about these strange people, he begins to come to the conclusion that despite the fact that they are almost universally called by one name, and that almost always they seem to inspire fear in the minds of better-known tribes, they themselves are not, in reality, a tribe at all.

What has happened in the course of centuries is probably something like this: In every tribe, from time to time, criminals or rebels or others who could not remain within the tribe, have escaped or been driven to take refuge in the mountains. Having broken the tribal laws, they might have faced death had they remained. Nor could they take refuge, often, with other similar tribes. Thus the no-man's land of the mountain fastnesses offered them their only possible escape, and to this no-man's land they went, ultimately peo-

OUR TURKANA RECEPTION. At first it was rather hard to photograph the Turkanas because most of the men wore no clothing; but we soon solved the picture problem by giving them calico to wear.

CAMP ON LAKE RUDOLF'S SHORE. Vern and Bob tried to sleep under the wings; but Osa and I gave up trying to sleep in the tent, for every night it was blown down by the sand storms. In the morning everything was covered with half an inch of sand. Nights were horrors, and days almost impossible, with the terrible heat.

pling it with a scattered population of friendless, ill-reputed groups who feared the natives of the plains below and did not hesitate, from time to time, to pick off wandering hunters or others who might, occasionally, leave themselves open to attack.

Furthermore, having lived for scores of generations in this manner and having increased only slowly in numbers through the appearance among themselves of newly escaped criminals and others, they have actually, because of the constant cross breeding of the various strains that make them up, come to have certain characteristics of their own, justifying, at least to some extent, the use of a name that seems to have certain tribal connotations.

Whether or not this is entirely sound anthropologically I do not pretend to say. But it is, I believe, a more or less accurate, if simplified, explanation of the Ndorobo people.

Now we, at Ngronet, soon heard, from Samburus, Rendilles, and Turkanas, certain vague rumors of the local Ndorobo, and thinking that an opportunity might well be at hand, we tried to get some of the local natives to entice a few of these wild men of the mountains to our camp. But we made no progress. The local natives would come to our camp, eat our food, accept our gifts, look casually at our planes, our flashlights, our cameras—listen to our phonograph, sell us goats' and camels' milk, and do a variety of other things, but bring in any Ndorobos they would not.

Each night from our camp we would see the light of dozens of fires in the mountains, and often during the day thin columns of smoke would be visible. Osa thought this smoke meant signals, but I doubt it. I think it merely meant that the natives were keeping their fires alive by using green wood, and green fuel smokes more than dry.

Once or twice we heard faint long-drawn-out shouting from away up in the valleys, the sound drifting down to us on the wind. All of this was very intriguing, of course, and we wanted to go up there. But the stories of poisoned arrows and Ndorobos waiting in ambush, of pitfalls covered with light branches and leaves, of deadly spears attached to heavy logs and drawn up in the trees ready to fall when an animal or a person walked underneath and tripped an invisible light cord across the trail, kept us from making the trip. And again, every day we expected the rains to start, for the sky was daily covered with heavy clouds and occasionally a light sprinkle would fall. Beside that, a trip up into the mountains would have been a hard one on account of the canyons and deep dongas. Furthermore, we did not have enough porters, and the Rendilles and the Samburus would perform no such menial tasks—they would not even carry a waterbottle or a gourd—they made their wives do that. Anyway, we felt that if we should go off into the mountains we might miss the elephants, should the rains catch us days away, and, after all, our principal object was the big elephant migration.

I spent a large part of one day, however, ingratiating myself with a visiting Samburu chief in an effort to get him to help in the matter. I let him look in Osa's mirror. I permitted him to turn a flashlight off and on until the battery went dead. I gave him trinkets, and because he expressed a little interest in our plane, I enlarged at great length on the power of such machines, and on their ability to do things in the air that no bird could possibly do. And finally I got around to the purpose I had all along in mind, and asked him if he and some of his men would go up into the mountains and bring in a few Ndorobos.

His reply was at first somewhat evasive, but when I pressed the point, he pointed to the plane.

"Why do you not fly your indagi—your great bird—up to the mountains and get the Ndorobos for yourself?" he asked. "You tell me it can do many more things than the birds can do."

"Why, it can," I replied, without at all realizing what I was walking into, "but the mountainsides are covered with trees. We cannot land there."

"But the birds," he replied. "The birds do not let the trees keep them from going to the mountainsides. They sit upon the branches."

And he turned away, obviously disbelieving every word that I had said in praise of airplanes.

It was about this time, too, that something happened that intrigued my interest still more in these wild folk, and made me still more anxious to photograph them.

As I have said, we had hired two Rendille tribesmen, with seven camels, to make two round trips daily to the water hole, in order to keep our camp supplied. I do not exaggerate when I say that the water that they brought was a filthy mess, as can be imagined from the fact that the water hole was always, except for an hour or so at dusk and an equal length of time in the morning, the gathering place of innumerable camels, sheep, and goats by day, and fewer, though still many, animals of the wild at night. Its filthiness, however, affected us not at all, for we have had much experience with water holes and had come equipped with a still by means of which perfectly pure water was daily distilled from the terrible stuff that came down to us by camel back.

We had arranged with the two Rendille natives to bring two loads of water a day, and for days they kept to that schedule. Sometimes they tarried on the way, to be sure, and were very late getting in with their second load, but they always managed it somehow, until the day I have in mind. On that occasion they started off as usual and we forgot them completely until lunch time, when someone commented on the fact that they had not returned.

"They'll be along soon," I replied, confident that nothing much could have occurred.

But when one o'clock and two o'clock passed without a sign of them I began to wonder if, perhaps, something had gone wrong. It occurred to me that they might have got into trouble with some of the herdsmen, perhaps, over some question of precedence at the water hole. And having thought of that I sent a boy off to find out.

He was gone, I suppose, the better part of an hour and

when he returned, breathless from having run all the way, all we could get out of him was just one word.

"Ndorobos!" he gasped. "Ndorobos!"

Just what the Ndorobos had done we could not learn immediately, and not wishing to delay in case there had been a fight and our Rendille natives had been killed, I called together half a dozen of the best "boys" we had, told them that there had been trouble with the Ndorobos at the water hole, and ordered them to get there as quickly as possible in order to help if they could, and at least to prevent more trouble. Osa, Vern, Moreno and I were to follow, armed, of course, and with a camera which my camera boy was to carry, in order to rescue our Rendilles, and to photograph the Ndorobos if we could.

The six boys who were sent ahead did not seem any too enthusiastic about their share in the work, but they were accustomed to white ways, and knew that if we followed with our guns they would have support so effective against the mountain savages as to put them to immediate flight. Consequently, they set off at a brisk trot, as we prepared to follow more slowly, and soon disappeared up the tortuous trail.

We hurried up the trail as best we could, but three miles of turning, twisting, rocky way, with the grade always up and steeply up in many places, did not allow us to make much speed. Still, for once the endless bands of camels and goats did not clutter up the way, and that helped. It told us, however, that something had very definitely upset the herdsmen, with the result that we wondered all the more just how serious this Ndorobo scare really was.

And when, at last, we arrived at the water hole, it was to discover a dozen or more native herdsmen carefully guarding their livestock in a little side valley, while they peered on up the rocky slope and chattered constantly among themselves. Our men were nowhere in sight, but neither were there any dead or wounded about. That, at least, was encouraging, and so we tried to learn just what had taken place.

The story, as it came from these excited herdsmen, and later from our own boys, was as follows:

Our Rendille water boys had arrived at the water hole as usual, and had proceeded to kill more time than enough, sitting about and talking while the herdsmen watered their stock. The seven camels that carried our water were hobbled in the usual manner—that is, one front foot of each of them was tied up by a scarf or band of cloth to the beast's upper leg. Thus handicapped they could hobble about on three legs, but could travel neither far nor rapidly.

For an hour or so, consequently, the seven camels were left to their own devices, while their owners sat lazily about the water hole, telling, no doubt, of the queer doings of the half-mad white people in the camp three miles down the valley.

Now, quite unknown to the herdsmen or our water carriers, the Ndorobos of the near-by mountains had crept down toward the water hole that day for some purpose of their own, and, hiding among the rocks and bushes, ready to seize any opportunity that offered, found that the seven hobbled camels were searching farther and farther up the valley for the meager remnants of parched forage that remained. While the camels were reasonably near the water hole nothing whatever happened, but when they had put a couple or three hundred yards between themselves and their owners, the Ndorobos apparently decided that the time for action had arrived. At any rate, quite to the amazement of the natives about the water hole, six or seven silent and rapidly moving figures suddenly materialized among the rocks near which the camels had strayed, and all in a moment cut the cloth hobbles and started to drive the frightened beasts on up the valley at the very fastest pace they could manage.

Just what happened next I never could make out from any of the stories that came to us, but I suspect that there was much shouting and excitement among the herdsmen and our two men at the water hole, but not much real effort to recover the stolen camels, owing to the fear that the Ndorobos inspired.

Fortunately, however, the valley above Ngronet waterhole does not permit of driving camels at any breakneck speed. The result was that when we had talked a few minutes with the herdsmen at the waterhole, and had decided to follow our boys, who now numbered eight owing to their having been joined by the two camel drivers, we had to clamber for only another mile or so before we made out the

47

camels that had so lately been in the possession of the Ndorobo camel thieves.

Now, exciting as all this was at the time because of the dangers that our imaginations supplied, I realize that it misses being highly exciting in the telling. My reason for telling it at all is rather to cast a little light on these little-known and probably misunderstood Ndorobos. That all the other natives are frightened to death of them is the simple truth. But when these terror-inspiring wild men were followed by a party of natives hardly superior in numbers to themselves, but who apparently showed some determination in the chase, the Ndorobos abandoned their loot without the faintest sign of a struggle, and disappeared hurriedly among the rocks and shrubs on a steep hillside. Our men later admitted all this in their more lucid intervals when they were not recounting their amazing prowess in regaining the camels.

Consequently it seems to me reasonable to conclude that these "bad men" of the mountains are not quite so bad as they have often been painted—that the wild Ndorobos are merely another group of Africans who, could their confidence be gained, would be likely to demonstrate characteristics not greatly different from the other better-known and slightly more fortunate natives of this same fascinating land. But, of course, this one experience with the Ndorobos was the only contact (if it is proper to call it that) that we had with them during our stay at Ngronet waterhole, and it is not impossible that my conclusions would undergo some change if I really knew a little more of these black wild men of the mountains. 48

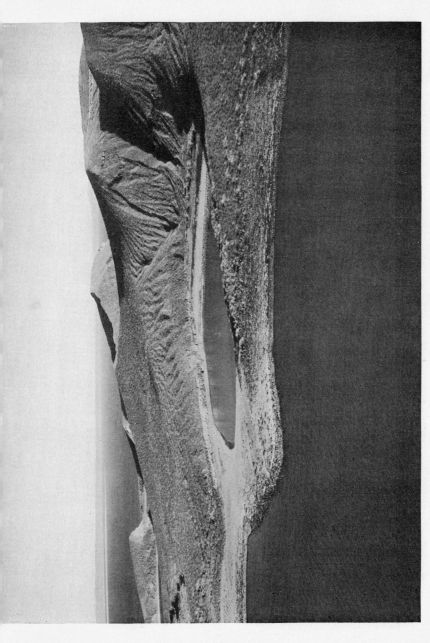

CRATER LAKE. Crater Lake on Center Island in Lake Rudolf. There are three lakes on this small island, full of fish and crocodiles, and attracting a wide assortment of bird life. The lake-water is very alkaline; and it is surprising that there is any life here. We could find no evidence that human beings had ever lived here.

MEN OF THE ABYSSINIAN BORDER. These are Borans, of the type who lived along the southern border of Abyssinia, where they have preyed on other tribes and other tribes have preyed on them for hundreds—perhaps thousands—of years. They are a good-natured bunch of rascals when at peace; in fact, it is probable they would never war on the other tribes if other tribes didn't start the trouble. Since they live so far from Abyssinian governmental headquarters, the Government has little control over them. This is why they are always in trouble with the British in the Northern Frontier and the Italians in Somaliland. Many tribes of the Boran have moved

3

OUR prolonged stay in the valley at Ngronet gave us an excuse to explore a region that, because of its aridity and heat, is very rarely visited by white men at any time, and gave us a new side light on the always interesting continent that has fascinated us for so many years. I have explained that Ngronet is only sixty or seventy miles from the southern end of Lake Rudolf, and it was the islands and the shores of this lake that attracted us. After all, sixty or seventy miles is only thirty or forty minutes by air, though the trip we took kept us away from Ngronet for a full two weeks.

Lake Rudolf is one of four huge lakes that lie in a long, irregular line some distance inland from the coast in Eastern Africa. Lake Victoria, Lake Tanganyika, and Lake Nyassa are the others of this group, and while they are all larger than Lake Rudolf, they differ in other ways as well. Lake Victoria is, of course, the source of the Nile, and about it lie some of the most beautiful regions that we have seen in Africa. Lake Tanganyika, long and narrow and forming a large portion of the boundary between Tanganyika Territory and the Belgian Congo, is another lake almost equally lovely, which is said to be the longest fresh water lake in the world, measuring, as it does, a little over 400 miles from end to end. Here and there about this lake enormous cliffs rise for thousands of feet abruptly from the water. Oddly enough, though the water is fresh, there are occasional periods which sometimes cover several years, during which the lake has no outlet. Years of somewhat heavier rainfall, however, soon raise the lake level until the excess waters flow across a bar and by way of the Lukaga River to the Congo and thence to the Atlantic Ocean.

Lake Nyassa, still further to the south, feeds the Shire River, which, in turn, enters the Zambezi and so delivers the waters of this huge lake to the Indian Ocean.

But to return to Lake Rudolf—while Lake Victoria forms the source of the Nile and so discharges its waters northward into the Mediterranean—while Tanganyika periodically sends its waters westward by way of the Congo to the Atlantic—while Lake Nyassa supplies a principal tributary of the Zambezi and so sends its waters southward and eastward to Mozambique Channel and the Indian Ocean—Lake Rudolf lies, without an outlet, remote and alone amid its desolation, greedily accepting the limited flow of the periodic streams that feed it, and giving up its waters only through evaporation under the burning heat of the equatorial sun.

Where the other great lakes in eastern Africa have towns and villages on their shores, with beautiful forests and plains all about, Lake Rudolf is without a single town— without a pleasant bay—without a redeeming feature. Its salty expanse lies amid an arid and desolate wilderness, where only the scantiest of vegetation manages to cling to the parched and wind-swept soil, where the mountainsides are devoid of trees, where furnace-heated winds seem almost endlessly to sweep across a land that would appear to be too harsh and desolate to support life in any form whatever. Yet, despite the heat, the parched earth, the dry stream beds, the salty water, and the fearful aridity of this region, people live there—pitifully ignorant and terribly unfortunate people who, luckily, know too little to realize how pitiful they are. If it were possible for them to appreciate the extent of their misfortunes, I can imagine that even they would not remain, or, perhaps, would fall upon their own spears in order to end an existence so utterly and irremediably hopeless.

Now even from the meager description I have given, it will be easy to understand why Victoria, Tanganyika, and Nyassa should be well-known, often-visited lakes, and why Lake Rudolf has very rarely attracted visitors to its shores. But the very reasons that impelled others to visit in pleasanter regions, impelled us to wish to explore the inhospitable shore line of this most inhospitable lake, especially as Ngronet waterhole was within so short a flight of the lake's southern extremity.

Osa, Vern, Sanial, Moreno, Davis and I made up the white contingent during the Lake Rudolf flight, and though the distance was not great, we had our hands full almost every minute we were away.

Over African Jungles

We left Ngronet at dawn, and in half an hour were over the southern end of Rudolf. The lake stretched ahead of us for almost two hundred miles, but to right and left the parched and mountainous shores crowded in upon it, holding its width down to a distance across which we could always see. Hills and mountains stood on every side, but seemed almost as bare and lifeless as the craters of the moon, though later, when we landed, we found that even in so desolate a waste scattered vegetation manages somehow to exist.

Ahead of us we made out an island of which we had been told, and which, if possible, we wished to visit. It is inhabited, but by a people almost too strange, if my information is correct, to continue to live in this strange world. They are Omolos, I believe, but for how long they have lived on this desolate island they call home I do not know. The only expedition (an English one) that has visited them, however, reported that they have no boats and consequently never visit the mainland, with the result that they believe that they are the only people in the world which, of course, does not exist, so far as they are aware, beyond the limits of their vision.

These pitiful people make crude little crafts of reeds, and so manage to paddle a little way from their island in order to fish, but their reed floats become water-logged so soon that a voyage to the mainland is an impossibility.

You can see from this that we were anxious to pay this island a call, for here was material sufficiently new to war-

THE BIG BABOON. This big baboon was bored at being photographed so often. A colony of these beasts happened to be near our camp
and we would often throw out food to keep them in the vicinity. They
became so tame that we could photograph them without using a blind.

LANDING SCENE. Landing in front of a Kikuyu village. The natives had been dancing and were so frightened that they tried to crowd into one hut, causing it to bulge out and collapse. Afterwards their curiosity became so great that we had trouble preventing them from doing the same thing to the plane.

rant attention. We watched the place eagerly through our glasses, consequently, as it grew more and more plain across the lake.

It took us little enough time to reach it, of course. Within an hour of the time we had taken off from Ngronet we were above the island, and I was taking pictures of it from the air. Vern, however, showed no signs of landing and after he had circled once or twice about the place I asked him why.

"Better not try it," he replied. "The water's too rough."

"Rough my eye," I replied. "It isn't rough at all. Look at it."

"That's what I've been doing," replied Vern. "Look. Watch the breakers on the beach. You can't see waves from the air much better than you can see hills."

And sure enough, when I scanned the beach with my glasses, I could make out plainly the foamy crests of waves as they broke and ran far up the sand, before dissipating and gliding back again.

I shook my head. Here was a disappointment, of course. Still, there were other things to see about Lake Rudolf, and perhaps we could stop and call upon "the only people in the world" when we returned.

Off we flew, consequently, to the west of north, with the great lake stretching out and out ahead of us, and growing longer and longer behind—with the parched and desolate mountain peaks to right and left, and not a white man in ten thousand of those desolate square miles.

Another hour's flight, or a little more, and we spied

another island—Centre Island. We had heard of this one, too, but no people inhabited it. Instead it is an extinct volcano, and within each of its three extinct craters is a little lake. Furthermore, as we circled the place, even Vern agreed that the water was quite all right for landing. Down we came, therefore, in a huge plume of spray, and presently had taxied up until the big plane's nose gently touched the beach.

We had heard that there were crocodiles on Centre Island, but not a crocodile was visible when we stepped ashore. Still, that was not surprising, for the beach was no fit resting place for crocodiles, devoid, as it was, of everything but sand and rocks. We had noticed, however, as we had circled overhead, that the crater lakes were ringed about with reeds and other vegetation, and one of them lay hardly more than two or three hundred yards from us across a steep little ridge that could be climbed without much difficulty.

We led ropes ashore from the plane, consequently, and made them fast to rocks upon the beach, left two of the "boys" who accompanied us as guards, lest the wind come up and carry our plane away, and armed with guns and cameras, climbed the slope intent only upon the little lake ahead.

And it was worth the climb, for no sooner had we reached the crest, beyond which the little body of water lay, than we saw that we had not been misinformed. Herons were there by hundreds, wading in the water, flying over it, or standing sedately amid the low vegetation on its banks. Here and there the pink plumage of a flamingo showed plainly in the vivid sunlight. But presently we saw all along the shore, wherever the reeds and shrubs did not obscure them, ones and twos—tens and dozens—scores and hundreds of lazy, motionless, ugly, horny crocodiles.

Now crocodiles had for years been no novelty in our lives. We have seen them time and time again. We had seen big ones and little ones and medium-sized ones. We had seen them singly and in groups, and now and again had seen them climbing and wiggling and writhing over each other until I think it is fair to say that we had seen them in heaps. But never, in all our lives before, had we seen crocodiles in numbers comparable to those we saw that day.

There were giant fellows napping in the sun. There were medium-sized crocs, seemingly almost torpid. There were little ones hurrying to and from the water or lying quietly in groups. For half an hour we watched them, and then, having found a place of vantage for my camera, I set it up and photographed crocodiles to my heart's content. Having made hundreds of feet of film, we threw stones at them and shouted, and filmed them still more as they scurried and twisted and hurried splashing into the water, while the herons, wondering, no doubt, what strange creatures had come to upset their normal scheme of things, rose and squawked and wheeled about overhead.

But an hour or so of this in the broiling sun was tiring, and presently I decided that I had earned a rest. I hunted up a nice smooth rock, therefore, that, with its overhanging edge made a comfortable seat, sat down and pulled out a cigarette, while still I watched the herons and the crocodiles.

Just what happened next I do not to this day know. Perhaps, subconsciously, I heard a sound beneath my rock. Perhaps, before I seated myself, my eye had caught sight of a suspicious shape or movement. At any rate, I had hardly lighted my cigarette before something impelled me to get to my feet and look beneath the edge of the rock that I had chosen for my seat. And when I did my heart leaped straightway into my very throat, for there, with its vicious head within six inches of where my right foot had been, lay the most gigantic puff adder that it has ever been my privilege to see.

Snakes, I must explain, are far from common in Africa. We almost never think of them when we are in camp. The natives almost invariably sleep on the ground, and though we have seen snakes from time to time ever since we made our first safari on foot fourteen years ago, they are so rare as not to give us a second thought.

Yet there beneath that rock lay the puff adder, its vicious head as big as my two fists—its great body as large as a man's thigh. Why it permitted me almost to put my foot into its mouth I never will know. Why it lay there so silently when I sat down over it I do not understand, but the truth is that it made no attempt to harm me, and we, in turn, did not harm it.

These venomous creatures do not grow to great length. Rarely do they exceed five feet, though this one seemed to

THE GREAT HERDS. There are 148 elephants in this herd which we photographed over the Lorian Swamp in the Northern Frontier district of British East Africa. During the two hours we were making these pictures, we passed over a score of herds, some of them containing as many as five hundred elephants. Unfortunately the air was very bumpy and it was almost impossible to get clear pictures. We were surprised that the elephants were frightened by our airplanes only when we flew directly over them.

SHOOTING A RHINO. Movie enlargement. Osa allowed the rhino to walk past her until he walked into her wind. Then his head went up, he made a few short steps forward, and, with head lowered, he came for her. There was about twenty feet of space between them when she brought him down. He had a large festered wound in his side which probably made him more aggressive than he would have been ordinarily.

CLOSE-UP OF RHINO. One of the best rhino pictures I have ever been able to get. This fellow had charged forward but, at the last moment, had changed his mind about attacking the plane.

me to be even larger than that. But for downright danger I give you the puff adder, together with the advice that you see that he keeps his distance.

We were ashore on Centre Island for three or four hours, and spent all but a few minutes of that time on the shore of one of the crater lakes. It lay, of course, in its own little depression, surrounded on all sides by the steep slopes of the ancient crater in which it had formed. It was well protected, therefore, from the wind which, during the time we had been away from the plane, had risen from the gentlest kind of a breeze to almost half a gale. As we topped the crest on our way back we felt it strong in our faces, and a glance at the plane told us that trouble was ahead, for the waves were sweeping in from the lake in greater and greater force, lifting the plane, pitching it about, and now and then driving its hull crashing onto the beach. Where the plane lay, fortunately, the beach was sandy. Had one of those plunges brought the hull down on any such rocks as were scattered about, there is no doubt that the light structure would have been broken.

We broke into a run, of course, piled our cameras and guns into the hull, hauled and pushed and struggled with the plane until it was turned about, soaking ourselves in the tepid salt water in the process, and finally had it in such a position that the motors could be started. But our troubles were far from over.

The waves, by now, were running really high, and an airplane is hardly the most seaworthy ship in the world. Such pitching and tossing as we went through in the next ten minutes is beyond my power of description. The plane stood steeply on its tail each time a big wave swept under, and came down with such a crash upon the next as to convince us that the hull could never stand the strain. Huge sheets of spray shot high over the wings. The windows ran with water, the wings and struts were dripping. Every article within the plane that had not been made fast was tossed and pitched and tangled into what a sailor would call a "hurrah's nest," while we, holding as best we could to anything to support ourselves, watched Vern as he slowly opened up the motors that gradually took us farther and farther from the island. Such crashing splashes of water I had never seen before—or thought I had not—for here we were, in a cockleshell of a hull, made top-heavy by the great wingspread and the two big engines that were supported on struts well above the level of the hull.

We could see almost nothing through the spray-laden windows, and we were in constant fear lest some more than usually heavy crash might set the hull to leaking—might weaken the support of the tail—or possibly might strain the supports of the engines which were slowly speeded up as we drew farther away from the beach and the seas grew a little less boisterous.

And now Vern opened up the motors still more. For a moment the crashes and the pitches seemed to increase, but as the plane gathered speed they seemed, somehow, to grow suddenly less. They were more rapid, though, and shook the whole craft. But now it was definitely increasing its speed. The crashes became a series of rapid hammer blows as we struck wave after wave in rapid succession. The spray still flew in a blinding sheet, but as the roar of the motors grew stronger and stronger—as the speed of the plane grew greater—we ultimately came to have more or less the feeling that we were riding over a corduroy road in a springless wagon. Then for a moment the pounding ceased. We had left the water. But—crash!—we struck again, and then— and every one of us, I know, took a breath of relief—we were in the air.

I saw Vern ease himself a bit at the controls, and could plainly see him as he relaxed.

"A bit rough, wasn't it?" he asked.

I don't believe any of us answered him, but it wasn't at all because we disagreed.

And now here we were, above Lake Rudolf, with no desire at all of descending on it again while those waves continued to run. We could, of course, have turned about and returned to our landing field at Ngronet, but we had planned to be gone for a week or two, and had no desire to be forced back after a mere half day of exploring. But neither did we want to use up too much petrol, for Lake Rudolf is not the best place in the world in which to purchase more. It consequently became necessary for us to find some sheltered bay, if such a place existed anywhere about that barren shore line, where we could land and haul the plane up onto solid ground, beyond the reach of waves.

Our map showed no such bay, but we knew, of course, that maps of such regions are more apt to be wrong than right, and seeing, to the west, a sort of blunt promontory that jutted out toward Centre Island, we turned and headed for it. We reached it in an extraordinarily short time, for the wind was "on our tail," and to our immense delight, we found a little bay which, lying in the lee of that headland, offered half a square mile or so of smooth water upon which Vern immediately landed. The beach was muddy, but in another moment he had taxied the plane up until its nose grounded softly in the shallow water.

The shore line, and the hills about, were almost as devoid of vegetation as one imagines the Sahara Desert to be. There was literally nothing, save here and there a tuft of dried and wiry grass. One could not imagine a more desolate place, or one in which it was more certain that natives could not be found.

"Well," remarked Osa as we opened the hatch and stood surveying the desolate shore line before us, "I see we're here, but will you tell me why?"

Vern grinned.

"To spend the week-end visiting friends," he announced, looking about over the lifeless shore line.

I don't think I said anything, but pulled out a cigarette and struck a match. For the moment, however, I forgot the match was lighted, for a quarter of a mile up the beach, half hidden by an intervening rise, I saw a group of black figures. I stared at them until the match burned my fingers, and then, in an attempt to be nonchalant, for none of the others had apparently seen them as yet, I lit my cigarette.

"Quite right, Vern," I agreed at last. "And here they come to welcome us."

And there, sure enough, they were—in plain sight by now—twenty or twenty-five utterly naked Turkanas.

They came on toward us with no hesitation whatever, nor with anything more, apparently, than the mildest kind of interest. It almost seemed to me that airplanes landing on their shore seemed completely natural to them, despite the fact that I knew that in all probability they had never seen one before and may never even have heard of such a thing. They were Turkanas, obviously, and one of the "boys" we had with us could speak their language. Consequently, when they had come up, he asked them to carry us ashore, where-upon they unhesitatingly waded into the water, took us on their shoulders and deposited us quite gently beyond the muddy beach on dry ground.

Still, however, there was no great interest shown in the plane. We were much more interesting to them, and they chattered more than a little among themselves, touching our clothes and smiling, or pointing to our faces and obviously laughing at the ridiculous fact that several men and a woman should be white.

Vern was as interested in them, of course, as the rest of us, but he is a natural born pilot and thought first of the plane. He had no desire to have the wind shift and create another situation such as the one from which we had just escaped at Centre Island.

"They'll help us pull the plane up onto the beach, Vern, if you want them to," I suggested.

"It isn't necessary," he replied. "I'll take off and land it on its wheels. It's level enough, and the sand looks good and firm back a way."

And off he went to attend to his task, while the rest of us remained with our new-found friends, wondering what they would do when the motors started and when the plane soared into the air above their heads.

But our wondering did us little good. We never in the world could have imagined that they would act as they did. Instead of being frightened by the roar of the motors—of staring in amazement as the plane took off—of standing open-mouthed as it banked and turned and swept overhead, they hardly gave the thing the slightest glance. Even when I spoke to them and pointed to it above our heads, they only smiled, glanced politely up as if to humor me, and turned their attention to their mild chattering and to us.

And when the plane came roaring down, and had finally rolled to a stop, they noticed only one single thing about it, and that was that the wings cast a broad shadow on the ground—a shadow that was rare and welcome in that sun-dried and largely treeless region. And having seen the shadow, they promptly took advantage of it, squatting or lying on the ground beneath the broad wings, without otherwise paying the slightest attention to this great bird that had brought the odd white people to their land.

With this beginning we thought that our jaunt to the shores of Lake Rudolf was going to be a huge success, and so it proved to be—with reservations—but we had about as disagreeable a time for the next two weeks as we have ever had in Africa. Though neither Osa nor I would willingly give up the memory of our visit to this desolate country and its people, we are not contemplating another visit.

The trouble, however, lay with the heat and the wind— not at all with our naked friends, and during our first day even the wind was mild. It was that, I suppose, that kept us staying, for having seen one day during which the wind did not half smother us in its clouds of dust and sand, we optimistically imagined that such another day would be with us with the next rising of the sun.

The local Turkanas were, of course, our major interest. The men were all utterly naked when we arrived, though the women wore abbreviated little skirts of tanned skins or bark cloth. But the plane had been prepared with natives in mind, with the result that before we left almost every member of the tribe had a piece of calico that was all his own, and the naked fellows blossomed out in "costumes" that were still quite scanty enough, but that managed, for all that, to effect an enormous change in their collective appearance.

It was perfectly extraordinary to see how little the plane impressed them. They glanced at it when it arrived, and then, apparently, ceased utterly to have any curiosity about it at all. Vern took one of them up, together with one of our "boys" who acted as interpreter, and when they landed, the fellow stepped out as if nothing whatever had happened. Vern told us, too, that while they were in the air he had tried to get his passenger interested in what was below them on the ground, but though the fellow looked out, he showed no interest. Then Vern had the interpreter point down and say "tree" as they passed over a gnarled tree that stood alone on the plain below. But the Turkana shook his head.

"No," he replied. "That is not a tree. You look up to see a tree, and you can walk under a tree, but we are above that thing down there."

His reaction was not different when a cow was pointed out to him. He insisted that it was not a cow "for a cow has legs," and, of course, from the air no legs were visible.

They were perfectly willing to help us set up camp, and when we wanted to move the plane a little way in order to get it into a more protected position, they turned to with a will, pushing and sweating in the happiest sort of spirit. But when I asked their chief if he wouldn't like to have a plane like that he assured me that he would not.

"The shade it makes is very nice," he told me, "but it is too hard to move, and we must go far to get food for our flocks."

Apparently the only value the plane had in his mind, or in the minds of any of them, was as a giver of shade in an overheated land very largely devoid of any shade whatever.

OSA FISHING. Osa fishing on the Chania River. Every stream and lake in Africa is full of fish; the scenery is beautiful; the climate perfect.

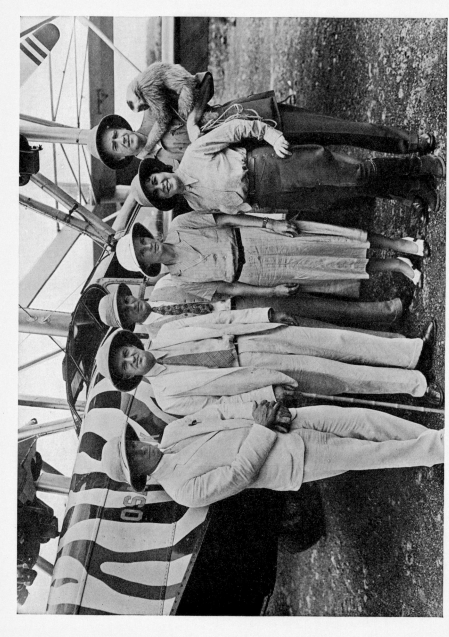

MEETING FRIENDS IN AFRICA. We met the Trubee Davisons in Kisuma on the shores of Lake
Victoria Nyanza and flew them to Nairobi. Left to right: Bob Cook, F. Trubee Davison, Kay C.

These Turkanas, like others of their widely scattered kind, have long, kinky hair, and have a custom which I have not run into among any other people. Like other natives they plaster their hair with mud and mutton tallow, and mold it into all sorts of fantastic forms, but their own particular custom adds another detail to that. A son, upon the death of his father, cuts off the paternal hair, and with plenty of mud and tallow, molds it into his own. Thus some of them had several layers of hair from dead ancestors plastered and daubed onto their own. The shapes these coiffures take are often perfectly extraordinary. Sometimes a huge slab of mud-and-tallow-daubed hair hangs down a man's back in a great beaver-tailed shape more than half as wide as his shoulders, and an inch or two thick. Sometimes their hair is arranged in grotesque and almost indescribable shapes, while one fellow had his arranged with a sort of handle, until his whole head, from behind, looked for all the world like an old-fashioned jug. When, to this detail, is added a generous daubing of alkali, making great, cadaverous patches almost anywhere on their bodies, the effect is certainly unique, even without the feathers that sometimes stand stiffly erect from the tops of their heads, the great ornaments, as large as one's hand, that are often suspended from their noses, and the lip plugs of ivory or wood, stuck through their lower lips in such a way that they can be pushed forward into sight or pulled back by their tongues.

There was a miserable little village not far from where

we had landed, and we visited it several times, but certainly it was a pitiful place. In a big circular wall of thorn bushes, through which, every fifty feet or so, there was an opening, were about thirty circular huts, each set close to the thorn wall. In reality, of course, this "wall" was merely a pile of thorns, and was, aside from that, not a structure at all. The huts were of wattle, daubed with mud and cow dung, while the whole middle section of the circle, which was, perhaps, a hundred or so yards in diameter, consisted of inadequate little garden patches, and small thorn-surrounded corrals in which their herds were kept at night.

But *such* a country! We set up our tents happily enough, and staked down the plane—not that we thought it was necessary, but merely as a precaution, and we had no sooner gone to bed that night than we learned how the wind can blow on the shores of Lake Rudolf. We were up half a dozen times before midnight, in order to fasten down the flapping canvas or in order to add new ropes to the plane. The gusts of wind already had the air filled with great clouds of dust, while the blowing sand cut our faces and got into our eyes each time we ventured out. Then the cook tent blew down, in a flurry of flapping canvas and rattling pans. We hurried out in order to smother the billowing canvas, and when we had made a bundle of it on the ground, we had to hurry back to keep our sleeping tents from blowing down as well.

The dust in the air, by now, was almost as thick inside the tents as outside, and our blankets were laden with it. It permeated everything before we finally left—chop boxes, clothes, food, cameras, guns, binoculars—and we ourselves were coated with it—begrimed—gritty—while every bite of food we took set our teeth on edge because of the sand and dust that it contained.

We got little enough sleep that first night, but daylight saw some diminution in the wind, so we set about cleaning things up—setting up the cook tent—polishing up our cameras—cleaning ourselves. But the next night and the next and the next were just the same, with far more than enough wind during the day. The cook tent blew down so often that we folded it up permanently, and the other tents were down as much as they were up. The dirt on our belongings and on ourselves was deposited more rapidly than we could clean it off, and Vern, always with his thoughts on the plane, worked for hours every day over the motors, cleaning, cleaning, cleaning. He covered them with their canvas covers, and used every idea that he could originate to protect them from the dust that somehow seemed to be able to sift through joints so tight that anything else under the sun would have been kept out.

Had we been able to guess, the day we landed at that wind-swept capital of desolation, that we were in for any such siege, we certainly would have been on our way at once. But we did not know, and so we made camp. And each new gale somehow suggested to us that it was the last—that the weather would turn fine, and that we could begin to clean our belongings and ourselves, preparatory to enjoying ourselves photographing and studying the simple natives of the district. But that time never came. We fought the wind and heat and dust and stinging sand until we could stand it no longer.

Vern made one trip back to Ngronet while we were there, and brought back more supplies, with the result that when we came to leave we decided that it was better not to attempt to take everything and everybody with us at once. Bob Moreno, consequently, and two of our black boys were left behind, with Vern's promise that he would return for them the following day or the day after, and we bundled our dust-saturated belongings into the plane and took off, sorry enough not to have learned more of the friendly and willing natives, but happy beyond words at leaving that homeland of dust storms behind.

We flew to the north, until the end of the lake warned us that Abyssinia was ahead, and having no permit to fly in that land we turned about and flew south once more, planning to visit "the only people on earth" and then fly back to Ngronet. But the wind was worse, as we approached the south end of the lake, than it had been on our northward flight. Great breakers were piling white foam in long windrows on the beach as we passed overhead. As a result we merely circled the island once—our petrol was low by now—and headed back for camp, looking forward to clean blankets and refreshing baths, to comfort and clean food and a windless night in camp. Our visit to Lake Rudolf was over, and none of us regretted that part of it, at least.

OVER THE TANA RIVER. "Spirit of Africa" over the elephant country. One of the most interesting of our aerial safaris. Elephants would scamper to cover as we passed; crocodiles slide into the ooze; hippos snort and plunge into deep water; and, now and then, a herd of buffalo would stampede away in a cloud of dust.

ELEPHANTS IN THE BUSH. A herd along the Tana River. There were about fifteen in the herd, some very small babies and one very old bull. They saw us and stood in a line with their trunks up and ears out. For a few seconds it looked like a charge, but evidently we did not seem very menacing, for they turned and walked a few hundred yards away where they found shade and

Over African Jungles

The next day Vern, who is tireless when it comes to flying, took off at dawn on his flight to pick up Moreno, telling us to expect them back that afternoon. We had no doubt, of course, and waved him a casual good-by, expecting, within six or eight hours, to see him back in camp. He disappeared over the crest of the hills and we went about our camp tasks, happy in our belief that he would be back with Moreno by midafternoon. But midafternoon came and went without a sign of the plane. Suppertime came, and still no plane. The sun set, and we in camp began to worry. Certainly something had gone wrong, but what it was we could not guess. I can assure you, however, that we were able to imagine a thousand things—motor failure, with the plane tossing helplessly on the great lake—storm and a battered hull, making flight impossible—broken landing gear—a crash that might have been caused by anything under the sun—tragedy of a hundred sorts.

You can be sure that we did not sleep well that night, for though Lake Rudolf was hardly more than a hop by airplane, it was an almost impossible journey by motor truck, and a fearfully difficult one on foot.

Our other plane was snugly in the hangar we had built at Nairobi, so there was no help there, though Vern and I, with airplane difficulties in mind, had long since agreed that before setting out on any rescue expedition we would wait for twenty-four hours beyond the expected time of the plane's arrival. We waited consequently all the next day, scanning the sky constantly, and hoping every moment to hear the roar of the motors or to see the plane high in the sky above the mountains to the north. But no motors were to be heard, and no plane came.

But it is not to be supposed that we merely waited. We planned what we were to do, as well, and prepared for it. In the first place, within an hour after dawn on the following day, a party of our boys, with Boculy at their head, was to begin a journey on foot to the lake, and we planned their program for them carefully. Sanial and Davis were to take a motor truck and to attempt a round-about journey by a way that might have permitted them to get through, in the hope, also, of reaching Vern in time to be of assistance. Osa and I, on the other hand, with a couple of boys, were to take the other motor truck and set out for Nairobi, driving as hard and as rapidly as possible in order to get our other plane, with which we were to return immediately for an aerial search. These were the plans, and before we went to bed that night almost everything was ready.

It took me a long time to get to sleep that night, as I suppose it did the others, but finally, I managed it, for I was tired. But with the earliest morning we were awake and began our last duties before starting in the three separate directions our parties were to take.

There were, of course, the usual delays, but finally we were all but ready to start, when, faintly from the distance, the sound of airplane motors reached our ears, and in another moment we saw the plane as it came flying over camp. We broke the record from camp to flying field that morning, I am sure, and when we arrived, it was to find Vern, Moreno, the boys and the plane in absolutely perfect shape, though many signs of mud were on the men and on the ship as well.

Nor did it take long for them to tell the story, which was merely that in attempting to land where we had left Moreno, Vern mistook a stretch of mud for a stretch of hard-packed sand, and only by the grace of a very good flier's excellent luck did he manage to keep from tearing off the wheels and turning the plane over on its nose. Even as it was the machine was bogged down until almost a hundred Turkanas, aided by both motors, found it impossible to move it.

Thus it became necessary to send those willing natives out for miles in every direction in a search for logs with which to make a sort of corduroy road over which the plane could be dragged and pushed to solid ground. And what higher tribute could be paid to the energy and willingness of those Turkanas than to say that they accomplished that almost impossible job in a day and a half, many of them single-handedly carrying logs, so Vern told me, that two white men could not easily have handled, and carrying them for six and eight and even ten miles across that awful, over-heated, windswept land of desolation as well.

I have often said, in the past, that next to the pygmies I like the Turkanas the best of any of the natives of Africa, and I am glad to say the same thing here. It is not merely

that they are willing to work that I hold them in high regard. The pygmies refuse to work at all, and I like them too.
But the Turkana is a gentleman, within his limitations, as
he proved in this case, and I, for one, am glad to give him
credit.

CAMP IN THE ELEPHANT COUNTRY. Our camp along the Tana River. Hippos and crocodiles are in the river; elephants and buffaloes in the forests on the river's edge; lions roared night after night. Moreover, the interesting natives and the fine bird-shooting make this spot one of the most fascinating in Kenya.

MOORING THE PLANE. After each landing in elephant and rhino country, the planes were taxied to a spot where they could be tied to the trees. A fire was started and boys stayed to watch the planes; for should an elephant or rhino come up during the night, he might get too inquisitive and leave us with a wreck on our hands.

4

IT WAS time, after our prolonged stay at Ngronet, for us to go elsewhere about our business of photographing animals. We had counted definitely on photographing the enormous herds of migrating elephants, and now had been forced to realize that, owing to the failure of the rains, there would be no migration. That was to have been one of the major bits of the motion picture that we had in mind, and so we were forced to rearrange our plans.

We decided, therefore, to move to a region that we had visited some years before, and in which we knew that there should be some excellent animal "stuff." This region lies to the east of Mt. Kenya and a little to the south of the Guaso Nyiro River. The particular spot we had in mind, so far at least as our landing field was concerned, was Garbatulla, the trading post of an old friend of ours named Perera.

Perera is a native of Ceylon, speaks flawless English, and is so black that I have often thought him blue-black. He has been a trader at Garbatulla for thirty-five years, and expects, I believe, to remain there for the rest of his life, trading knives, sugar, salt, and calico for the skins of cattle and of sheep, for the rope made by the Somalis of the

73

region, for leopard skins and anything else that he can obtain. His expenses being very low indeed, he was able, after many years of trading, to accumulate a competence with which he planned to return to Ceylon. He turned his holdings into cash, therefore, only to have every shilling of it stolen on the night before he intended to depart. Ceylon, consequently, became an impossible goal, and he was forced to continue at Garbatulla where—for the world depression has visited even that out-of-the-way spot—business is not so good as it once was. The chances are remote that Ceylon will ever see him again, for to have saved enough at Garbatulla on which to retire was remarkable even when times were good. He is not likely to be so fortunate again.

Garbatulla, however, being nothing more than Perera's wattle and mud trading post, did not boast a landing field, and before we could use our planes in that vicinity a landing field was necessary. Osa and I, consequently, with Vern Carstens, took off for Nairobi with the films we had exposed at Ngronet and on Lake Rudolf, while Moreno, Sanial, Davis, and Fritz Malewsky, who had recently joined us, took our five motor trucks and, with thirteen native "boys," began the hard 300-mile trip across country to Perera's trading post.

While I was engaged in developing film in my Nairobi laboratory, therefore, and while Osa was busy getting together more supplies for another extended period in the field, the motor truck party was to go to Garbatulla, enlist Perera's help, and level off a space in that unusually level country where we, two weeks from the time we separated at Ngronet, could land the plane and begin our work anew.

We learned later that it took the motor party only five days to make their 300-mile trip—not bad, when one realizes that not a foot of this was over a road, and that most of it was over country devoid even of a trail, where innumerable abrupt banks had to be cut down, and other innumerable gulleys filled in before the trucks could pass. And, as luck would have it, Perera, on whom I knew we could count for help, managed to find nine wandering Turkanas, in this land of Somalis and Borans who will not work, to assist in the preparation of the landing field, and was able, as well, to find, in his little stock of trade goods, the necessary "jimbies" and "pangas" (that is, the hoes and knives) that the work required.

Thus it was that three hours or so after we took off at dawn from the Nairobi airport two weeks later (for we were using our big, two-motored plane and made better than a hundred miles an hour), we found ourselves over Garbatulla, while below us, and immediately in front of Perera's simple little trading post, we saw a thoroughly satisfactory field prepared for our reception.

In the meantime, too, Perera had thoroughly aroused the interest of the local natives in the expected arrival of the white man's "indagi," with the result that several hundred Borans and Somalis had journeyed in from 'round about to see an airplane for the first time.

We circled the field, located the "air sock" that had been

set up, and landed in a cloud of dust, to the astonishment of the assembled horde of savages, and were instantly welcomed not only by our own party but by Perera as well, without whose assistance the field most certainly would not have been ready. And Perera, whose business it was to learn from wandering natives every bit of news of the surrounding country, immediately told us that a group of Borans who had just arrived from the vicinity of the Lorian Swamp, a hundred miles or so away, had reported the presence there of unbelievable numbers of elephants.

Now elephants had long been on our minds, and this bit of news was just what I wanted most to hear. Osa, however, from long experience with natives, discounted the story, and even Perera could not swear that it was true. Nevertheless, I wanted to investigate, and so we filled the tanks of the plane at once, preparatory to taking off for a few hours in the air.

Osa, however, declined to go. We had already decided to pitch camp on the banks of the Kina River, forty miles or so to the south and west. The Lorian Swamp lay in the opposite direction two or three times as far. Consequently, Osa took charge of four of the five motor trucks, and with our thirteen boys, set off for the Kina River in order to set up camp, while the rest of us, with Perera as well, climbed into the plane, intent on elephants.

Seventy or eighty miles to the north of Garbatulla the Guaso Nyiro River flows eastward toward the Lorian Swamp, and it was to the Guaso Nyiro, in the vicinity of

a spot long known as Kittimaster's Camp, that we first
headed, for the members of our own motor truck party had
followed the Guaso Nyiro for a way, and told me that they
had seen a few elephants and rhino. As a matter of fact,
Sanial had risked his neck to take a close-up picture of a
rhino, only to find, after he had made the attempt, that
the camera had contained no film.

But now we were off, roaring over the parched country
and searching constantly with our glasses for some sign of
game, while Perera, from his seat by a window, marveled
constantly at the wonders of the airplane.

Who Kittimaster was, or when he camped beside the
Guaso Nyiro, I do not know. I only know that Kittimaster's
Camp is now only a name, and on this particular morning
its only inhabitant, so far as we could see from the air, was
a lone bull elephant that shuffled hurriedly away as we
flew overhead. Nevertheless, he was the first elephant that
we had seen, and he cheered us up. Consequently, we banked
and headed downstream toward the Lorian Swamp, hoping
that the report the Borans had made was accurate.

But now that we were flying down the valley instead of
over the plains, the air grew outrageously bumpy, and
Perera, unaccustomed as he was to flying, for this was his
first trip in the air, gave way immediately to an attack of
air sickness which lasted, unfortunately, during our four
remaining hours in the air. And now, too, we began to see
what we had come to find. Another elephant appeared in
an opening below us, and then we saw several. A herd of

buffalo galloped off, and a lone rhino ran about, wondering, no doubt, what extraordinary creature could make so much noise up there in the air. More elephants appeared—a herd of five—a herd of fifteen. The common game were everywhere, and we flew over a colony of baboons.

I was busy, now, with a motion picture camera while Hugh Davis, intent on getting still pictures, opened the hatch and stood with his head and shoulders out while Moreno and Sanial took turns holding him by the feet to keep him from being thrown out when we fell so sickeningly in the air pockets.

The river below us grew narrower and narrower, and by the time we reached a crossing called Merti it disappeared entirely, save for an occasional little pool about which the trampled earth told plainly of the animals all about.

For an hour and a half, I suppose, we flew over that dried-up river bed, banking and circling about now and then, when we came upon some unusual aggregation of animals, and I believe it is fair to say that never, from the time we saw that first elephant at Kittimaster's Camp, were we out of sight of the great beasts. At first they had been scattered, in ones and twos and threes and fours. Then we sighted them in dozens and scores, and finally, as we approached the edges of the Lorian Swamp, we saw, ahead, enormous flocks of white herons that told us, even before we saw the herds of elephants themselves, that the Borans had vastly understated the case.

I was photographing constantly now. A herd of a hundred or so elephants appeared beneath us, and as Vern banked and turned in order to permit me to photograph it, I saw scattered herds of even greater size as far as my eyes could reach. Never, in all my years in Africa, had I dreamed of seeing elephants in such enormous numbers. The great swamp was literally filled with them, and because of the utter lack of trees there was hardly a herd that we failed to see.

White herons flew below us in clouds, while below them the herds of elephants made their way through the swamp grass, trampling down enormous swaths in their search for food and water.

We flew back and forth over the great swamp for an hour, and in that time did not catch sight of any water whatever, so dry had the season been. Nevertheless, water must have been present among the dense growth of marsh grass. In normal times hippopotami are to be found in the Lorian Swamp. What, I wonder, becomes of them during such a period of drought?

We suddenly flew over a giant herd of elephants that must have numbered all of four hundred, and in the next twenty minutes we passed over six more herds nearly as large. Mere bunches of fifty or a hundred no longer seemed worth photographing, and not one of us could even estimate how many elephants there were in all. And, too, they did not seem unduly perturbed over the roaring thing that soared above them. They did not stampede. For the most part they hardly seemed startled. It was almost as if they felt that nothing in the world could equal the collective strength that they themselves possessed.

As a boy, in the West, I have often been impressed by the power of a herd of cattle two or three hundred—or possibly a thousand—strong. Even a herd of sheep, if it is large enough, can give one much the same impression. Imagine cattle or sheep, then, in thousands—two or three thousand, perhaps, or possibly more. The power they collectively possess is enormous. But imagine what we saw that day—not sheep or cattle, but elephants—giant beasts, each of which has such strength as makes a sheep or a cow seem as nothing. And imagine these vast creatures in their resistless thousands—two thousand or three—possibly more, for I do not know how many there were—and you have imagined such power as Nature rarely assembles among living things.

We were breathless with excitement. Many a time I have spent hours and hours trying to photograph *one* such beast, and here below us—in sight at one time—were more elephants than I had ever seen in all my life before. And Osa had not believed the story that had led us to them!

Back and forth and 'round and 'round we flew. I had taken thousands of feet of film, and now reached for another loaded camera, glancing at Vern as I did so.

He shook his head.

"We've got to be going," he remarked. "The gas is getting low."

I glanced at the gasoline gauge, and I don't know when

THESE TWO RAN. When Vern and I made our first flight to Tanganyika, to select a landing place, I bet him a shilling that we would see lions within five minutes. In three minutes, these two jumped up and ran across the plains. Vern never paid the shilling, saying I knew that I was betting on a sure thing.

KING OF BEASTS. This handsome lion was the largest and finest I have ever seen, both in size and mane. He was in the prime of life and looked every inch the "King of Beasts." Both he and the lioness watched every motion I made—they even consented to growl a little, so that an excellent sound record was made on the film.

I've been more disappointed. I could have photographed that breathlessly exciting scene forever, had gasoline and film been available.

"Can't you hang on a little longer?" I demanded.

"Better not try," he replied. "We'll have to cut across country now in order to get back."

I took up another camera, determined to get a few more feet, and nodded to him.

"Go ahead if you have to," I agreed, and turned to the task of exposing more film.

Vern banked and straightened out, examining his map and laying his course. We passed over the edge of the great swamp and headed out over the desolate, level waste of country that lay between the swamp and Garbatulla. Not a landmark lay in all that level stretch of tree-dotted land —not a hill or a stream or anything to tell us where we were. Only Vern's sense of his position and the compass could direct us now, and there was too little petrol left to permit us to fly back the way we had come.

Perera, too, was sick, poor fellow—deathly sick, and was too weak to help us. He sat hunched up in his seat, his honest black face had turned ashy in color, and his usually bright eyes were dull. And none of the rest of us knew the country over which we were flying, while a hundred miles lay ahead of us, with only a tiny collection of mud and wattle huts at the end to tell us where Garbatulla lay.

The petrol gauge dropped little by little, and still the characterless country spread out everywhere below—level enough, of course, but broken by trees and bushes among which we dared not land.

Vern, however, seemed confident enough, as he flew his compass course, and finally, after an hour of doubt, he pointed ahead. There, hardly two miles away, and directly on our course, lay Perera's trading post and our landing field.

We landed about two o'clock, had a hasty lunch, and within half an hour were in the truck that Osa had left for us and on our way to the Kina River. We made good time, too, for it was easy to follow the four trucks that had gone ahead, and the country was level. It took us only a little over an hour to reach the spot that Osa had chosen for camp, and what a beautiful spot it was.

The Kina River itself is a small stream, only twelve or fifteen feet in width, but flowing, as it does, down from the foothills of Mt. Kenya it is a marvel of beauty there at the edge of the dry-as-dust plains on which Garbatulla lies. Its water is cool and clear, the vegetation on its banks is green and bright, and Osa, who has a sense of the fitness of things, had camp almost ready, with the tents pitched near the stream beneath the wide-spreading branches of a magnificent and gigantic wild fig tree.

For the moment, however, the beauties of the camp site did not strike me, for only a mile or so before we had reached it we had seen a lone rhino well off to the side of the trail we had taken. One reason we were here on the Kina River was to take photographs of rhino, and, I thought, here was our opportunity to test out a theory that we had long since developed—a theory that the rhino's charge is apt to be a fake—that instead of charging home, the wrinkled brutes will tend to turn off if their pretended targets stand firm.

We jumped from our truck, therefore, and calling Osa, took an unloaded truck and immediately set out to find the rhino we had seen. Our luck was good, too, for within half an hour we located one, though whether or not he was the one we had seen before I do not know.

At any rate, we stopped the car at a safe distance, and when we had crept forward through the dry grass to a point at which I could set up the camera, Osa went on ahead a little way to see what would happen.

So far the rhino had not detected our presence, but a moment later he heard us or caught our scent, and went into action all in a moment. There was no foolishness about this fellow, who wasted little enough time in snorting and none at all in trotting about. Up went his tail and down went his head, and theory or no theory, he came for us.

More particularly, he came for Osa, who, now, was standing twenty or twenty-five feet in front of the camera, with the intention, I know, of letting him charge up to the point at which his own better judgment would tell him to turn aside. And I must admit that he came at top speed. He had been all of a hundred yards away when he started his charge, and without deviating an inch he came pounding toward Osa, who stood quite still awaiting him.

I had turned the switch on the camera even before he started, and I watched him eat up the distance between them. Once again I was impressed by the power of the great beasts, and knew all too well that, if our notion of what he might do was wrong, Osa would have to shoot. Furthermore, she would have to use all her ability as a marksman, for he was getting close, and a miss might make anything possible.

I wonder, sometimes, just how gigantic a rhino would seem if one should find oneself facing a charge at a distance of inches. We have been quite close enough, many times— forty feet, thirty feet, and on one or two occasions twenty feet or less. I know that even at those distances a rhino looks fantastically gigantic. But what, I wonder, would one think of such a beast at twenty inches?

And that, I suspect, was in Osa's mind, too, for she was twenty feet or more closer to the galloping old fellow than I was, and was standing there quite bravely, too. He was within twenty yards of her, by now, and still he showed no signs of turning off. Still, we had not expected the charge to prove itself a fake at that distance. On he came, still at top speed, and suddenly Osa fired. I saw the bullet strike— saw the animal stumble to his knees—saw him stagger up, run a few steps off to one side and fall.

Osa stood for a moment watching him, but he didn't move and I saw her shake her head. Then she turned and came toward me, frowning.

"I'm sorry, Martin," she remarked. "I'm sorry I shot

WILDEBEEST ON THE SERENGETTI PLAINS. This was a small bunch, the first of the big migration that came along a few days later when the plains were covered with millions of head of game . . . yes, I mean millions. No other place on earth offers such enormous masses of wild game as these Serengetti Plains.

LIONS IN THE MORNING. A typical morning scene on the Serengetti Plains. The three young lions are in the prime of life, the lioness is young, another lioness was sunning herself just outside the picture.

when I did. I think he might have turned away, but he looked so big that I got buck fever."

We went back to the truck, intent on trying to find something else, for the light was still good, and driving off through a patch of bush we came, presently, into a large, park-like area a mile or so wide and all of four or five miles long. It was almost entirely open, and we spied five rhino as they moved slowly into the open space from one side.

Here, we thought, was an opportunity to get a highly unusual rhino picture, for one does not often see so many together. We stopped the car, consequently, in the shelter of a tree, and moved forward slowly with the camera.

Between us and the five unsuspicious rhino lay a steep little donga that we would have to cross, and moving as quietly and as carefully as we could we started toward it. But in the donga, entirely hidden from us, were a mother rhino and her awkward baby, and we, despite our care, were coming closer and closer to them as we advanced. We were still at some distance from their sheltered spot when they scented us, and all in a moment a huge snort stopped us, while a slightly lesser snort echoed the first. Then, in a rush, both mother and offspring bolted away, up the farther side of the donga and directly toward the five rhino that we had hoped to photograph. And now they, too, took alarm. With a series of snorts all seven rhino took to their heels, and away went our chances of a highly unusual photograph.

The light, by now, was failing, too, and the day was

about over, so far as photography was concerned. We returned to the truck, consequently, and with Osa at the wheel, started for camp.

I was in the back, packing my camera into its case and putting things to rights as Osa wound her way in and out among the bushes, and was paying no attention whatever to what lay ahead, when suddenly, and without the slightest notice to me, she slammed on the brakes. There was a screech of straining brake drums and the car stopped abruptly, pitching me among cameras and film cases, water bottles and guns. I banged my head badly, and extricated myself with some difficulty, angrily wondering what under Heaven had happened and why I had been so pitched about.

The others were pointing and talking excitedly when I pulled myself up to look, and there I saw still another rhino galloping off among the bushes.

"What happened?" I demanded.

"We nearly ran into him," Osa replied. "He came around that bush right there."

And there, sure enough, were his tracks, less than twenty feet ahead of the car.

The rest of the way to camp, thank goodness, was uneventful. I had a bump on my head that was caused by my being thrown down among our paraphernalia, and anyway, I had seen enough for one day. To have left Nairobi only that morning, to have seen literally thousands of elephants, to have had a rhino charge, to have missed photographing seven rhino in one group, and now almost to run another rhino down was, I suspect, the fullest day I have ever spent. It had all been thrilling, you can be sure, but even thrills can come too rapidly. For one day I had had enough.

Camp was all in order by the time we returned to it, and after our prolonged stay at Ngronet this spot beside the Kina River seemed absolutely flawless.

There were seven tents for us, in addition to four or five that we had for the boys, and arranged, as they were, along the bank of that beautiful stream, beneath the long branches of the enormous old fig tree, they made a picture of comfort. Osa, too, inveterate fisherman that she is—had already located a pool only a little way above camp where, for dinner that night, she caught a dozen or so delicious fish. I have long since given up trying to decide which of our many camps has been the most delightful, but certainly, if this one on the Kina River was not preëminent, it ranks very, very high. But it was not until early the next morning that I noticed one of the most beautiful things about it.

We had had a full day, of course, and we were tired, with the result that we all went to bed early. As for myself, I went to sleep immediately, too, and hardly moved until morning, but suddenly I awoke, when the faintest light of early dawn had only begun to show through the tent top above me, and never before, I believe, have I heard so many birds singing at once. I slipped out of the tent noiselessly, to stand before it and listen. Then it was that I saw hundreds upon hundreds of weaver bird nests hanging from the trees all along the stream, some built on slender branches that let them sway only a little way above the water, and everywhere the weaver birds were singing as if to burst their throats. There, I can assure you, was an alarm clock that would make anyone want to get up. And as I watched and listened, Osa appeared behind me. What, we wondered, has civilization to offer that is half so wonderful as such a morning in the "wilds of darkest Africa"?

For several days we had no particular photographic luck, and because we were still afraid the rains were on the way we did not want to stay too long, beautiful though the camp site was. Dry weather was one thing in this district, but the rains would have made it impossible for us to get our trucks out, and would seriously upset our program. We worked constantly, therefore, in an effort to photograph what we could, so that we could move on, and every day we watched the huge masses of clouds as they piled up and up in the clear sky, expecting at a moment's notice to break camp and beat a hasty retreat to Garbatulla.

But though, for a few days, we were unsuccessful photographically, Osa was fortunate with her rods and lines. Almost every day she found time to fish, and on one occasion she brought in a two-pound perch, while on another she caught a ten-pound catfish. Still, it was her fishing that nearly got her into serious trouble one day.

The stream, as I have said, was not large, but it was impossible to follow it for any distance without going back of the trees and brush that lined it. This Osa soon learned, and it became her custom to go upstream a way, until she

A FAMILY OF LIONS. A family group, consisting of an old grandmother, two full-grown females, and ten half-grown cubs. Some of them were in the bush in the background when this picture was made. It was an affectionate family, playing all day long like a bunch of puppies.

LIONS AROUND THE PLANE. There were thirteen lions, but we could not get them all in the picture because they were constantly coming and going. Lions pay no attention to the human form if they can see it only from the waist up. Had Osa stepped onto the ground, they would have run away *or* they would have attacked her . . . but probably the former. Several times, while the plane was here, the lions licked it with their tongues.

found an opening—a game trail perhaps—leading to the water, and there to approach the stream and fish for a time before moving on to a similar spot beyond. On one of her trips she had gone about her fishing in the usual manner, and finally had come upon an unusually narrow way leading to the water. Watching her rod and line carefully, consequently, in order to keep them from tangling in the branches, she made her way down to the bank without, I suspect, looking about her very thoroughly, but as she prepared to cast, she heard a rustle and a movement behind her. She looked about quickly and was startled to see a crocodile coming swiftly toward her down the narrow place through which she had just passed. How big he was I do not know, and I suspect that Osa's surprise prevented her making any very accurate estimate of his size. Anyway, he was quite large enough to be decidedly dangerous under the circumstances, and Osa leaped into the bushes, willingly giving him the right of way. He passed her in a rush, and slid into the water, while Osa decided that she had had fishing enough for one day, and returned to camp where she told me the story.

It was interesting, too, that crocodiles should have been in such a place. They usually seem to prefer the warmer, muddier streams, yet the Kina, at least while we were there, was both cool and clear. However, it empties into the Tana only thirty or forty miles from where we were camped, and Osa's crocodile had very likely come from there.

About this time, too, we had another experience with a

charging rhino. The whole affair was almost a duplicate of the charge we drew on our first day there, and once again, despite her determination not to do so, Osa fired when the old fellow had come up to about thirty feet. She hit him on the horn, this time, and he turned and galloped off quite as rapidly as he had come, but Osa was angry, even without the comments that I made.

"I didn't mean to shoot so soon," she insisted. "I really didn't. But when they are coming that way, they look a whole lot closer than they really are."

And to that I heartily agreed. One's imagination cuts the distance down enormously.

I do not remember now (and my notes do not tell) whether it was before or after this that we had an experience with a rhino there in camp, but for a moment the beast's visit created its own share of excitement.

The boys had erected a sort of table made of forked sticks stuck in the ground and light poles laid across them, and on this our varied assortment of pots and pans was kept. The whole thing stood, perhaps, four feet above the ground, and it made a most convenient addition to the cook tent.

We were all asleep one night when, with no warning whatever, we heard an enormous clatter of pots and pans, of breaking sticks, and of extraordinarily energetic rhino snorts. We leaped from our beds, instantly seizing our guns as we did so. Dashing from our tents, we were just in time to hear the snorts and the trample of a rapidly retreating rhino, which, investigation later proved, had blundered into camp, and had, oddly enough, gone squarely under our rack of pots and pans. Naturally, the structure was completely wrecked and our cooking utensils were scattered about. We considered ourselves fortunate under the circumstances, however, for certainly he had chosen the most effective possible method of awakening everyone.

Not far from camp we found a small swamp, and we soon learned that rhinos often came there to drink. We put it on our list, therefore, and visited it almost every day. Usually the rhinos appeared at this favorite spot late in the afternoon, and we tried to arrange our calls so that we would be waiting when they arrived. In this way, from a carefully chosen spot in the shelter of three big mimosa trees, we managed to photograph several rhino. On one day, however, we found, to our surprise, that a rhino was already in the swamp when we arrived. Furthermore, we had taken no particular care to approach quietly, with the result that the old fellow heard us.

I have already commented on the fact that a rhino can move more rapidly than his appearance would suggest. Nevertheless, I did not believe that any rhino could move rapidly through such a place, bogged down, as this one was, to his knees in mud and water. But no sooner had he heard us than he took to his heels, and he seemed to go just as rapidly through that mud and water as he could have done on dry land. The mud flew in great black sheets, and the water was churned into spray, all but hiding the beast as he fled. Even before I could begin to photograph him he was gone, while still, along the path that he had left in the swamp, the churned-up mud and water showed plainly the course that he had taken.

We came to know the country 'round about very well indeed, for we went out every day with a motor truck and cruised about for fifty miles or so. We had to do most of it in low gear, too, for the country near the Kina is not like the plains that lie a little way back from it. The result was that our radiator was boiling most of the time that we were out, and the cars were under a tremendous strain. But it was worth it, for the country was filled with game. Buffalo were not uncommon, and we saw small herds of them on several occasions. Rhino were really numerous, and we saw ten or twelve or fifteen almost every day, though the tick birds that always accompany them usually gave us away before we could get the cameras into action. There were many rhino mothers with their babies, too, and elsewhere in our experience that has been far less common.

Once or twice, too, we saw elephants, but they were not numerous. Lesser kudu and zebra were common, however, while kongoni, bush buck, and water buck were usually about. We saw no lions whatever, and only two or three leopards, though cheetahs were plentiful. Baboons were really numerous, and monkeys were everywhere, on many occasions actually coming brazenly into camp.

Here and there in the more heavily wooded sections we saw signs of the local Ndorobo, for they very commonly built platforms in the trees and there lay in wait for animals to pass below. By this method they are able to spear animals that they might otherwise not be able to come upon in wooded country.

We were constantly afraid, as I have said, that the rains would begin and make it impossible for us to take our trucks back to Garbatulla, with the result that after far too little time on the Kina, we were frightened into leaving by an unusually impressive display of gigantic clouds. We broke camp hurriedly in the face of this threat, and congratulated ourselves over having done so when, having arrived at Garbatulla, the heavens seemed to open. The rains, we thought, had certainly begun, and we were fortunate to be away from the Kina River country.

We chuckled over the matter that night, I recall, as we sat snugly in our tents beside the flying field, and I recall thinking how fortunate we were to have escaped when I went to bed that night and listened to the drumming of the rain on the tent fly.

When I awoke, however, the sky was clear, and not another shower came our way. Still, we were not to be caught by returning, for we had made plans to meet an expedition sent out from the American Museum of Natural History, in order that we might help them collect four elephants with which to complete a museum group. We packed up our belongings, consequently, took leave of our friend Perera, and took off for our return to Nairobi.

The American Museum expedition consisted of Trubee Davison, the president of the institution, his wife, Dorothy, and Pete Quesada, a United States Army pilot. None of them being familiar with Africa, they had arranged for Al Klein, one of the very ablest white hunters in Africa, to accompany them and handle their safari. Their purpose, as I have said, was to complete an elephant group which is to be the central exhibit in Akeley African Hall at the museum, and while shooting does not mix well with photographing, Osa and I had been asked to go with them and we were glad to be able to do so.

Al Klein had made all the necessary arrangements for the safari, which was to go to the Tana River, but Osa, Dot Davison, and I decided to let Trubee and Al go ahead with the nine motor cars, with the extra large number of porters that the expedition required, and with the ten skinners who were hired to handle the elephant skins. Trubee could have waited and gone with us as well, but he wanted a closer view of the country than we would get from our plane, so off he went with Al and the motor cars.

We gave the motor party three days to reach the little government post of Garissa, and then, early one fine morning, we took off and followed. Dot Davison and Pete Quesada, with a native cook and quantities of baggage, used our smaller plane, "The Spirit of Africa," while Osa, Vern Carstens and I used "Osa's Ark," in which we also packed two natives and most of my cameras.

It was a beautiful day and we saw lots of game, from the moment we left the Nairobi flying field. Even before we reached the Tana River, too, we saw elephants in a patch of thorn bush country, and a little later we saw several large herds in the forests along the river.

We found the little government station at which we were to meet the motor party, and found, too, that the flying field that had been built there by the District Commissioner was entirely satisfactory. We landed promptly, consequently, and found not only that the motor party had arrived, but also that an old friend of ours, Captain Sharp, whom we had known years before at Marsabit near the Abyssinian border, was the commissioner for the district. It was he who, realizing that troubles with the wild desert peoples of the vicinity might otherwise be difficult to control, had had the Garissa flying field built.

So far everything had gone according to plan, but our next move necessitated a crossing of the Tana River which, as luck would have it, was high. We had to spend a couple of days, therefore, hiring all the native canoes in the vicinity, in binding them together with logs and bamboo, and finally in creating a ferry capable of taking our over-burdened trucks.

Once that was done, however, finding a camp site was easy. A few miles upstream, at a beautiful spot near a bend in the river, we made camp, and now our daily work was to hunt for the four elephants that the museum required.

An inexperienced person might imagine that such a project would be easily completed in a region where elephants were as numerous as they were there beside the Tana River, but difficulties lay ahead. The reason the job was not an easy one was that Carl Akeley, years ago, had collected the giant bull that is to dominate the museum group, together with a lesser bull, a cow and a baby. Now it had become necessary to add four more to the group without interfering with the dominance of Akeley's huge bull, at the same time completing a small herd that would be typical and truthful. Thus big bulls were out of the question. Also mothers with young must on no account be killed, and as luck would have it, though we saw elephants every day, they were all too rarely of the size that must be obtained. The elephants that were required had to be slightly smaller than full grown, and by the strangest of eventualities, we found mostly handsome big tuskers.

It consequently became our task to examine every herd with the utmost care, before making the slightest effort to go further, and we spent more days than a few following elephants, watching elephants through our binoculars, choosing just the elephant to get only to learn in time that that particular beast was a female with a baby in the herd, and otherwise using up more time than enough. Osa and I, too, cared little enough for all this, for we were passing up literally dozens of excellent opportunities for photographs.

Day after day we wandered about that country, looking farther and farther for the beasts the expedition had come to get, and finally we went so far from camp that it was necessary to sleep out beside the Tana River.

We stopped at the edge of a dry stream bed, beside which

LIONS AT A ZEBRA KILL. This family of lions had fed and fed until they could hold no more; but they were reluctant to leave their zebra kill. A short time afterwards, they collected in small groups and licked the blood from the faces of one another.

THE LION STARES. Two enlargements from movie negatives. Note the expression on Osa's face as she and the lion stare at each other, and her expression as the lion turned and left. This was almost an everyday occurrence after the lions got used to the plane.

THE LION LEAVES. Our experience has always been that wild lions are very curious and, after a few days, overcome their fear of strange objects. One day a half-grown lioness placed her forepaws on the side of the plane and, pressing her face against the glass, looked in at Osa.

the trees and vines stood in an almost impenetrable mat, and found a number of places where the animals had torn the vines and trampled the earth until they had created veritable caves in the dense growth. The roofs and walls of these were mats of vine-covered branches and trunks, and they offered excellent shelter for our cots.

The Davisons chose one of these, and Osa and I took another somewhat further from the river bank, and across the little donga through which the narrow and dried-up stream bed meandered. We got our cots out of the motor truck, made them up, put our guns carefully in place beside us, and turned in, cozy as anything in those tightly tangled jungle "caves."

We were tired, too, after a long day bumping about on our search, and I, at least, went instantly to sleep, as I believe Osa did as well. But quite suddenly I was awakened by the cracking of branches, and sat up instantly. The moon was shining brightly overhead, and I remember trying to determine about what time it was, as if that made any difference. The crackling branches, however, soon broke off that line of thought, and I could see, by a tiny bit of moonlight that filtered through the mat of vegetation overhead, that Osa was sitting up as well. I had already taken up my gun and could see that she had also.

So there we sat, as silent as we knew how to be, gripping our rifles and wondering what to do next, for as yet we had not the slightest idea what was creating the noise. The crackling came again, and even the vines above us moved.

It was all very strange, and then, quite clearly, I heard the rumbling of an elephant's stomach.

It is an odd thing that that sound can be so plain, yet it is. Despite that, however, it can be heard at no great distance—a hundred feet, perhaps, or a little more. Of course, as every elephant hunter will tell you, it is a definite sign that the elephant is contented, and by that much is encouraging, yet even a contented elephant seems a bit too close when he is within a hundred feet of your bedside. Still, what were we to do? I tried my best to see through the vine-clad bushes, but they were so dense that the moonlight had little opportunity to penetrate them.

Now and then a vine overhead would tighten and snap, as a branch a little way off was broken, and presently a particularly vigorous pull set the whole roof of our jungle room to swaying, showering us with leaves and twigs. That, I must say, seemed too much for us and we both crept silently from our cots, holding our guns ready, of course, and, once outside our jungle bedroom, beat a hasty retreat toward where the Davisons had set up their cots.

We found them asleep, too, but we awakened them and told them the story, whereupon we all sat with our guns in our hands, talking in low tones, until the feeding elephants had moved off farther into the jungle. Once we felt that they had gone far enough, we went back to our cots, shook the litter of leaves and twigs from our blankets, and went back to bed. I never had heard of an elephant eating up the walls of one's bedroom before.

98

Over African Jungles

The first elephant secured for the museum was killed by Dot Davison. We had been following a herd for two hours or more when our elephant trackers, who were a long way ahead, came back to us and reported that the elephants had turned about and were now headed toward us. We pushed forward, consequently, hoping to see them in some fairly open spot.

In this we were fortunate, for when we saw them they were among some bushes above which their great backs showed plainly. We paused and studied them for twenty minutes before Trubee and Al Klein decided that one was just the size that was needed, and agreed with Dot that this, the first elephant, was to be hers.

No sooner had this decision been reached, either, than the beast stepped out into clear view about seventy feet away. Dot fired at once, but the animal seemed only to be wounded, and in case of a charge we would have been in a bad situation, with the undergrowth so thick. Consequently both Al Klein and I fired as well, but our assistance had not been needed. The elephant went down, and when the others had stampeded, which they did at once, giving us a chance to go up to the dead animal, we found that Dot's bullet had been the fatal one. Al and I had fired because the elephant had not gone down immediately, but elephants often stand for half a minute or more, even when they have been struck vitally.

Later Trubee brought down the second elephant in circumstances almost exactly similar, and a day or two after that they dropped the elephant hunt in order to search for specimens of the rare Hunter's hartebeest which the museum needed. While they were thus engaged, consequently, Osa and I remained behind to do some photographing, for that is always our business when we are in the field.

The hartebeest specimens, despite the rarity of the species, were obtained promptly enough, and when the Davisons had returned, the elephant hunt was completed quickly as well, though in shooting the fourth—a young bull—a big bull charged and had to be brought down as well. In the excitement and danger, too, Trubee caught his foot and fell backward, knocking Dot over as well. I was not present and did not see the excitement, but for a few minutes there must have been more danger than enough. And there was one more dead elephant than enough, as well, for four was all the museum had planned to use.

But now the museum's needs were satisfied, and after a few days during which the skins were prepared, we took off for Nairobi. We had other plans, now, and the Davisons were to be our guests on an aerial safari to the Serengetti Plains. There was to be no more collecting, save the collecting of photographs, for we were bound for the land of lions—the ones that we have called "the friendly lions of Tanganyika." Without a visit to this marvelous region no visit to the game fields of East Africa is even half complete.

CHEETAH MOTHER AND CUBS. After nearly sixteen years in Africa, this was the first time I have been able to photograph cheetahs at close quarters while they were conscious of my presence. On this occasion, I followed them for two or three hours and was able to make many pictures at a distance of 50 feet, although the light was very poor.

CAMP AT 10,000 FEET. A camp for the night on the slopes of Mt. Kenya. Clear and bracing air at this altitude made us feel that we owned the earth. We knew the bushes and forest near by sheltered countless elephants, rhinos, buffaloes, leopards, lions, and antelope. A thrilling safari land.

5

OSA and I have camped many times on the Serengetti Plains, but they cover a great area, and in order to locate a good camp site near which we could conveniently and safely land our planes, I thought it wise to make a preliminary flight so that our trip, when we actually made it, would go off smoothly.

Consequently, at daybreak one beautiful morning, Vern Carstens and I, in "The Spirit of Africa," the smaller of our two planes, took off from the Nairobi airport, and headed south.

The day was wonderfully clear, and from the plane we could see to the distant horizon in every direction. It hardly seemed possible that we were flying at a hundred miles an hour, so great were the distances. It appeared, rather, that we were merely floating through the clear air, beneath the blue sky and above the endless, quiet plains. We seemed merely to glide above Lake Magadi, the great soda pan that, from the air, looks so like the country about Great Salt Lake in Utah. White as snow beneath us, scores of smooth square miles lay vividly in the sunlight, with mirror-like pools of open water scattered here and there. On to the south we flew, over the rounded shoulders of a mountain. Beyond that lay a ragged stretch of rocky plains, and finally we sighted the beautiful little park of mimosa trees around and outcropping of giant bowlders where, many times, Osa and I had camped while we photographed and explored in this fascinating region.

All about this spot spread the seemingly endless Serengetti Plains—hundreds of square miles of gently rolling country, cut, here and there, by some slowly flowing, tree-lined stream. The prairies of Kansas and Nebraska must have been very similar to this section of Africa when, before the settlers came, they were peopled only by scattered bands of roving Indians and by the herds of game.

But here on the Serengetti Plains the game is still present —visible in every direction as far as the eye can see. Great herds of wildebeest, of zebra and kongoni. Countless head of topi, impalla, and giraffe. Eland, too, were everywhere, mixed with Thompson's and Grant's gazelle, ostrich, warthog, waterbuck, baboons, monkeys, and scores of others. From long experience in this region I knew that in the wooded dongas were lions, leopards, and cheetahs, while herds of buffalo must be somewhere about, and a dozen kinds of buck and antelope must certainly be in the patches of tall reeds.

It is, I suppose, all but impossible for any person to visualize this country without seeing it. Even I, who had spent months wandering about among these always-present herds, was astounded at the countless animals we saw as we looked from the plane. For years I have been a frequent visitor to the Serengetti Plains, and, with our motor cars, have driven almost everywhere about their great extent. Yet from the air that day I saw more game than I had ever seen before.

Vern, of course, was excited. Why shouldn't he have been? I had told him of the game of this most favored region, but I had vastly understated the case. I had, however, promised to show him lions, and he reminded me of that.

"All right," I agreed. "Fly down over that little wooded donga."

He did as I suggested, and within two minutes of the time that I had spoken, two lions jumped into sight and hurried away.

On we flew, and presently saw others sunning themselves in the open. There were ten or a dozen of them—a big male, a few lionesses, and several youngsters. Half a mile further on a big group of graceful roan antelope trotted lightly along the slope of a small hill. Here, certainly, was Africa as God made it—to me, at least, the most interesting and thrilling land on earth.

Everywhere we flew we saw more animals and both of us, I am certain, could have flown all day, never tiring of the sights we saw. But the gas gauge, that controlling factor in every airplane flight, was telling us that we had little gasoline left beyond what we required for our return flight. So, flying low over the plains near our old camp site, Vern carefully inspected the ground until he found a place that seemed free of ant hills and pig holes. Then, watching carefully, he made his landing—perfectly, of course, as Vern always seems to do.

He had chosen an almost perfect spot, too, and immediately we set about marking out the limits of this new flying field of ours. We had brought scores of yards of white calico with us and now, after tearing this into strips, we spent two good hours whittling sticks, thrusting them into the ground, attaching our calico to them, and in this way marking the boundaries of a good, safe field.

By that time we were tired, so, choosing the pleasantest spot that we could find, in the shade of a tree, we got out the excellent lunch that Osa had prepared for us, ate it at our leisure, each took a nap, and then, about four o'clock, took off once more and flew back to Nairobi.

It seems odd to me, even after I have done it, that one can climb into a plane, can take off, and with the utmost ease, fly so many hundreds of miles in a day, still leaving time to pause, perform all sorts of duties, take leisurely naps, and still be back in time for supper. Africa is so amazingly huge, and the distances are so extraordinarily vast that it seems almost impossible to do many of the things that we, on our last expedition, did so much as a matter of course. When, as we did within a few days, we sent Fritz Malewsky, Bob Moreno and Hugh Davis off with our motor cars to the "flying field" that Vern and I had staked out, we knew that it would take them at least five days to reach it.

LAUGHING HYENA. Movie enlargement. Spotted laughing hyena with wildebeest in the background. Plains game pay little attention to hyenas, knowing they are harmless as long as they are in sight. The hyena usually attacks baby animals just born, or finishes the bones of kills left by lions or leopards. Any active antelope can outrun a hyena.

SNOW ON THE EQUATOR. The peak of Mt. Kenya; altitude, 17,040 feet. Standing exactly on the equator, it is covered in snow the year round and has several permanent glaciers. Kenya is not one of a range of mountains, but one distinct mountain protruding from the plains surrounding it.

We actually gave them seven, before we took off again by plane. Yet Vern and I had been there and back in less than seven hours. Certainly the world has changed—even in Africa.

But now, a week after Fritz, Bob, Hugh and their troop of "boys" had headed for our proposed camp site, Dot and Trubee Davison, Pete Quesada, Osa, Vern, and I, in "Osa's Ark," our big plane, took off and followed. All along the way we watched for game, and our friends, quite naturally, were excited about it. Even Osa bobbed up and down excitedly as she pointed out this and that, for all the world as if even she had never seen game before.

Camp was quite ready for us when we landed. It only remained for us to move in. And at dinner that evening we constantly paused and listened, as the sounds of the game on the plains about us came drifting to our ears. Our dinner was excellent, as it usually is in camp, and our sleep that night, out there with the countless animals all about, was perfect. Surely, if one can only get away from the troubles and problems of economics and civilization, the world is beautiful yet.

We were naturally eager to get started—Osa and I because the country was so familiar to us—and the others because it was so new. In our best camera motor car, therefore, we started out immediately after breakfast on the following morning. Osa was driving, and had Dot and Trubee with her in the front seat, while Pete Quesada and I stood in the back, our heads and shoulders above the opening in the top of the car and our cameras ready to shoot.

Osa needed no directions, naturally. We had long since discovered the best places for lions in that vicinity. She took us, consequently, out across the plains, down the sides of a little valley, through a shallow stream, and up the farther bank to the plains once more. She was heading for a reed-grown donga that we had often visited, and presently she entered it, bumped along its length for two miles or so and —quite as if we had made arrangements in advance—came squarely upon two fine, sleek lionesses. They rose from the grass, looked casually at us, stretched, yawned, and sat down on their haunches to watch us, their faces kindly and their manner very mildly curious. They yawned occasionally, and their curiosity was so slight as presently to turn— or so it seemed—to complete boredom.

Our guests were naturally all keyed up with excitement. Who would not be on seeing their first wild lions in the heart of Africa? But the lions showed no trace whatever of excitement, and presently moved off through the reeds, lying down again where we could see only the tips of their ears.

It is a strange thing, this attitude of lions in Tanganyika. They pay very little attention to a motor car, or even to an airplane, as we later learned. They apparently do not view the occupants of a motor car as being separate from it. Many times I have sat on top of my camera car with my big professional cameras, have moved all about and made scene after scene with lions only a short distance away. I

have changed film and talked to Osa, and done almost anything else I cared to do, all without having them pay more
than the slightest attention, even to our voices. On the
other hand, should a person step from a car, and definitely
appear separated from it, these very lions will be off in a
flash or will charge with all the energy of which they are
capable. Usually, of course, they will run, for they live in
a country alive with game and in which, consequently, they
need not greatly exert themselves in order to obtain food.
The result is that they are not trouble hunters. They are
generally fat, sleek, and lazy. Often, no doubt, they are
muscle-bound, for they rarely take any great amount of
exercise. And of course they sleep a great deal, spending
most of their time lying around in the shade. In this they
are different from leopards and, I believe, from tigers.

Yet I do not mean to give the impression that they are
not dangerous, for they most certainly are. A lion is a powerful beast. His strength is huge. Yet, on several occasions,
I have had both lions and leopards charge and there is a
difference. A leopard comes like a streak of lightning and
is hard to stop. He is small, of course, and consequently not
easy to hit, but he can be filled with lead and will sometimes
still keep coming. He hugs the ground, and so perfectly do
his muscles coördinate and so swiftly does he move that he
seems to glide rather than to run.

The lion, on the other hand, is up on all four legs when
he is coming, and while he is graceful and fast, he has
neither the speed nor the suppleness of a leopard. But when

he reaches you and gets you down it is your finish, while I have known several people to fight leopards barehanded and still live to brag about it.

I have often been asked whether a lion or a tiger would win in a battle between them. I do not know, of course, and one is not likely often to see such a battle or even to hear of one, for there are no tigers in Africa, or lions in India, save for a few in a restricted area where they are protected and where tigers are almost, if not quite, unknown. My own belief, however, is that in the event of such a battle, the tiger would have the advantage, even to the extent of being all over the lion and of defeating him decisively. I believe that this has sometimes occurred where the two, in menageries, have occasionally fought.

But we were not thinking of tigers, there on the Serengetti Plains. Lions were what we wanted to see, and lions were what we saw, for Osa drove on down the donga we were in until, two or three miles farther on, we came upon two big taffy-maned fellows in the prime of life—great, powerful, beautiful lions, and with them a young, fine-looking lioness.

Out came our cameras, of course, and we began making pictures the moment Osa stopped the car at a distance from them of about a hundred and fifty feet. The lions paid little enough attention to us, however, and I told Osa to drive up closer, which she did, moving forward perhaps fifty feet. They still paid us no particular attention, and I suggested another move, which we made, stopping, this time, at seventy-five feet or so. Still, however, nothing happened. I was not, of course, looking for trouble, but those lions were really handsome, and I wanted them to drop their blasé attitude and do something, no matter how mild, so that the motion pictures I was taking would have at least a little movement in them.

Now Osa and I had done this sort of thing scores of times before, and many times had approached lions to within a fraction of the distance at which she had now stopped the car, so, quite without thinking that our three friends were new to this game and that they might quite readily view three entirely competent lions with certain qualms that were foreign to me, I told Osa to go ahead again. But Trubee, I more than half suspect, thought I was doing all this in order to show off, and he put a stop to it at once.

He leaned back and said in no uncertain words, "This is close enough, Martin." And from the half-angry expression on his face I knew that he was in earnest.

But there is really more to the story, despite the fact that we did not go closer, and contented ourselves instead with watching the beasts for a time before, at last, turning about and heading back for camp. What should be added is that before we had been on the Serengetti Plains for two weeks, Dot and Trubee went off alone one morning in a car, with the understanding that in an hour or so Osa and I would follow in another machine. And what was our surprise, when we followed, to find the two of them intently engaged in photographing a band of thirteen lions, some of which were within fifteen or twenty feet of the Davisons' car!

This being on the Serengetti Plains with an airplane at hand intrigued both Osa and me, with the result that we proposed a scouting expedition by air for the next day. Certainly the camp site that we had chosen was in good game country, but, we thought, a little trip by air might show us a better. Consequently we took off the second morning after we had arrived, and within half an hour or so were flying over the Duma River, fifty miles from camp. And as we had hoped, the game was greatly more plentiful, while, to make it more interesting, we sighted a large herd of buffalo.

This was too good to miss, so, having returned to camp after only a couple of hours in the air, we gave orders that camp was to move on the following morning to a delightful spot in a bend of the Mblanketi River, only a few miles from the Duma. Here there was good water for the boys and for us, after we had distilled it in our copper stills, while, all about camp, the plains were covered by tens of thousands of head of game, of more than twenty species. Almost at the edge of camp there were monkeys and baboons galore, and we soon learned that within half a mile lived a huge, black-maned lion and his family of four young lionesses, one old grandmother, and seven half-grown cubs.

We discovered this group the day after we arrived, and you may be certain that Osa and I were delighted, for, without any doubt whatever, the big, black-maned male was quite the largest we have ever seen in all our years in Africa, and, in addition, was one of the handsomest.

As I explained, we found them the day after we arrived, and hoping to get better acquainted, we shot a zebra, towed it up close to our new acquaintances, cut the rope, and drove away, having thus made our first friendly advances. Thereafter, every day, we did the same thing, and ultimately came to be expected when, with a good lion dinner, in the shape of a zebra, towing behind the car, we drove up to serve it.

Some might say, of course, that any such course is indefensible, but we do not feel that way about it. If we had not supplied the lions with food, they most certainly would have obtained it for themselves. Furthermore, we killed the animals instantly and painlessly, and many times we have seen lions bring animals down and even start to feed on them before they were dead. As a matter of fact, all the sportsmen hunters in Africa kill fewer animals in a year than the lions of the continent kill for food in a single night.

Obviously, then, with these lions so close to camp and with the tactics we pursued, we came to know them well. But the big fellow, almost as if he realized that he was a perfect trophy for some hunter, was anything but willing to show himself. The others were almost always in evidence, and we could generally tell where the big one was—could often see his ears, or a patch of his black mane as he kept in the background—but it was not often that we saw him clearly, as we almost always saw the others.

Over African Jungles

The chosen spot at which these lions were usually to be found was a sort of island about which the Mblanketi River spread two half dry beds. The river, when we were there, was not a flowing stream. Instead, its bed was mostly dry, with pools dotting it here and there, with the result that it was perfectly easy for our motor cars or the lions to go and come across the river bed with no trouble. The island itself (if such a tract can properly be called an island) was a beautiful, park-like place, covered with waving grass a foot or more in height, edged, along the stream beds, with big, wide-spreading trees, and dotted, at a distance from the stream, with palms, while clumps of palms were here and there about the island. At one end, too, the ground fell away into a small, almost dry swamp.

It was a wonderful sight to see this handsome pack of lions when, early almost every morning, we came to make our call. When they would see us coming they would get to their feet, yawn, stretch, and walk slowly toward us. If we had meat for them they would wait politely until we had left it for them, and then would settle down to breakfast. If we failed, however, to bring them anything, they would walk around, sniff the air, and then stand looking at us as if to say "What? No zebra?"

Of course, we were not bringing meat to them merely for the pleasure of feeding them. We wanted pictures. But often, when the sun was hot, they would drag the kill into the shade, which did not suit our cameras. Consequently, on one occasion, we killed a topi, towed it toward them, and

THE PEAK OF MT. KENYA. The peak on a cloudy day. It was in this area that Osa contracted pneumonia several years ago after we had climbed for many days to reach the snow line. Only a person with her strong constitution could have survived.

CAMP ON THE SLOPES OF MT. KENYA. In the Nanyuki district. Our airport is only a few hundred yards to the right; from here we cut a road so our planes could be taxied down to camp, as wild animals often walked through the airfield during the night. Here, at an elevation of nearly

while they were still at a safe distance, stopped and tied their meal to a dead tree which, being without either leaves or branches, gave no shade at all.

It was especially hot that day, and the lions—there were twelve of them—had no desire to feed there in the broiling sun. But though they made a number of efforts to drag the kill away, we had tied it tightly and the rope was strong. Then, almost as if someone had gone to him for help, the big fellow came walking solemnly out of the swamp, where we had not been able to see him, got the topi by the neck in his powerful jaws, gave several mighty tugs, broke the rope, and dragged the animal into the shade where the others immediately began their meal. The big one, however, having performed this task, did not take even one bite of food, but turned instead and marched into the swamp again, pausing just before he disappeared, and standing for a moment looking back. Never, I believe, will I forget that pose —power, serenity, confidence—Simba, the king of beasts. And once again he seemed to me to be the most magnificent wild animal that I had ever seen.

On another day we reached the island late, and the lions had retreated into the dense, shady bush near the swamp. Not one of them was to be seen. We cruised about looking for them, and stopped the car, presently, beneath the gaunt, dead branches of a huge, fallen tree. I was searching all about with my glasses but could see nothing, when Vern Carstens, who was beside me, nudged me with his elbow and pointed up.

There, on a big, bare branch above us and hardly more than five feet away, was one of the half-grown lions, watching us seriously. His head was moving from side to side as he followed our motions, and though he was utterly silent, he was obviously intently interested.

Naturally I was startled, but his face was so benevolent —so good-natured that, after I recovered myself, I almost felt as if he would have permitted me to reach up and pet him. (My urge to do so, however, was not so great as to cause me to try it.)

We had long since learned that lions do not fear motor cars. But we wanted to learn what they would do in the vicinity of an airplane. So Vern taxied "Osa's Ark" down into a small bushy donga not far from the "island" on which these lions lived. Then, when we took the next zebra to them we merely dragged it near them without leaving it, turned about and dragged it back across the dry stream bed and into the donga near the plane.

By now, of course, they had no fear of us, and despite the fact that the zebra was not left for them as the other kills had been, they seemed to know that it was theirs. The fact that it kept moving, however, puzzled them, and we had a most amusing time watching their efforts to stop it.

There was the zebra, at the end of a rope, thirty or forty feet behind our car, and there were the lions, all about it, trying to keep it from getting away. They tugged and pulled, but all to no avail. A youngster sprang upon the striped carcass and rode for two or three yards before half jumping and half falling off. Another did the same thing, and a third leaped on before the second fell off, but there was not a sign of anger. They were really quite pleasant about it, and even their guttural growls seemed to have no more anger in them than the playful growls of a dog playing with his master.

We towed the kill up to within sixty or seventy feet of the plane, let go one end of the rope, permitting it to slip from the zebra's neck, and drove off to a considerable distance, watching the feasting lions for a time. They paid no attention to the plane, and we decided to follow the same tactics on the next day, leaving the kill a little closer to the plane. By advancing in this fashion it was not later, I believe, than the fourth or fifth day that we had the lions unconcernedly feasting within twenty feet of the plane.

That, we figured, was close enough, and now Osa often got into the plane before we brought the kill up, opened the hatch on top, and standing on it, with her head and shoulders out sometimes talked to the lions which, on several occasions came directly up to the fuselage of the plane, and often wandered back and forth beneath the wings.

From the camera car, a little distance off, I took hundreds of feet of pictures of all this, but the lions were so numerous that we did not care to risk anything to excite them too much. It is all very well to play with these beasts as we played with them, but it never pays to forget that they are just as full of potential destruction as any stick of dynamite. In a flash any one of them could have turned from a great, pleasant kitten into a fierce and deadly beast, and we knew it. Consequently, as much as I wanted action, I took no unnecessary risks, and figured out no fool experiments.

And then, one beautiful sunshiny day when Osa was in the plane and Bob Moreno and I were in the camera car, while the lions lay about and yawned, I suddenly became conscious of the fact that a new lion was among these old friends of ours. He was a full-grown, taffy-maned fellow, sleek and beautifully muscled, and most certainly we had never seen him before. I realized that he was a newcomer before Osa did, and I wondered what would happen, though I must admit that I was not prepared for what came.

Osa was in the plane, as I have said, but knowing that I needed a little time to get my camera ready, she had not opened the hatch. But now, seeing through a window that my camera was set up, she slid back the hatch, thrust her head and shoulders through it and started to talk, as she had done several times before, to the lions outside.

But no sooner had her head appeared than this new fellow tensed and growled. And no sooner had he heard her voice than he charged. He was not more than fifteen or eighteen feet away when he started, and luckily Osa saw him at once. Down she dropped, slamming the hatch shut above her head, but she could be seen clearly through the heavy safety glass in the side of the plane. In an instant the lion crashed heavily against the pane which, fortunately, he struck at an angle. It was fortunate too that the pane was not made of ordinary plate glass, or that lion might readily have scram-

OSA'S CHEETAH PETS. Osa and her four baby cheetahs, the most interesting little pets she ever owned. All day they would wool one another about, sham-fight, follow us about. At meal-times they were always around the table begging; at night, tired out, they would sleep in their basket huddled up together; and, in the morning, they were up and in our beds, begging us to get up and feed them and play with them.

WAH. Wah, our gibbon ape from Borneo. We bought Wah just after he'd disembarked from a Borneo steamer, before we left New York. He made the entire safari with us and loved the airplanes; he learned

bled inside and killed Osa in the next ten seconds. As it was the glancing blow and the heavy safety glass corromed the beast off, leaving Osa unharmed.

I was frightened, I can assure you, and wished that we were well away from there. And naturally I thought that Osa would be unnerved as well. But what was my surprise, while the lion was still grumbling immediately beside the fuselage, to see the hatch slide gently back—to see Osa thrust her head carefully out—to see her raise her hand, with a missile of some kind in it, and see her, the next moment, throw whatever it was she had straight over the side of the plane at the offending beast. And then, as the missile struck, I realized what she had done.

Frightened, naturally, but angry as well, Osa had no sooner seen the lion crash against the window of the plane than she decided to teach him better manners. Consequently she seized the first thing that came to hand, which was, of all things, a cardboard carton of prepared biscuit flour. Opening the hatch she threw this deadly projectile at the villain of the piece, and, fortunately for me, my camera got every detail of the happening, even to the spraying flour that whitened the animal's yellow mane as he scuttled hurriedly away.

The lion was not frightened, of course, but he was puzzled, and going off a hundred feet or so he sat down, licked flour off his coat until it almost gagged him, whereupon he tried to clear his mouth of it by using his paw, and finally rolled in the grass.

But the package of flour had given Osa an idea. Consequently, having ducked inside the plane again, she reappeared, this time with a little frying pan. Before I knew what she was about she let that fly, and hit a young lion unexpectedly in the ribs. He let out a snarl and leaped to one side while Osa, suddenly vociferous, shouted at them and dared them to try any more charges until the whole group was definitely excited. They were looking about now—growling a bit, lashing their tails, and all the time Bob Moreno, busy with his sound equipment, was almost chortling in glee.

"Gee!" he remarked. "That's wonderful. Keep your camera going."

But there were too many excited lions about and another charge might break a window in the plane. The risk was far too great. Consequently, sound or no sound—pictures or no pictures—I shouted to Osa to close that hatch and stay inside until I could come and get her. But it was over an hour before the lions wandered off and I was able to do so.

There were, of course, many other things to do there on the Serengetti Plains beside play with our favorite pack of lions. We photographed wild cheetah in the open—the first time I was ever able to do so. We saw another pack of lions that numbered twenty, and one mother had two tiny cubs that climbed all over her and chewed at her tail and ears for all the world like playful kittens. In that group, too, there was a lioness without a tail, and we wondered if, by any chance, she might be the mature edition of a tailless cub that we had seen in much the same district five years before.

On another occasion Osa and I drove our car beneath the branches of a wide-spreading mimosa tree, and hearing a rustle overhead we looked up just in time to see a handsome leopard leap from among the leaves, lightly touch the top of the car and bound swiftly away. Further inspection showed us, too, that up there in that tree—fifteen or eighteen feet from the ground—was a full grown impalla, dead and wedged in a crotch.

We got out and examined the tree carefully. The lowest branch was a full eight feet above the ground, and it seemed an impossible task for a leopard to climb the trunk with any animal so comparatively great as an impalla. Yet there the dead animal hung, and nothing in the world but the leopard could have put it there.

It was, I believe, within an hour or so of seeing the impalla in the tree that I had an opportunity to do something very different indeed.

In the trees about camp orchids were not uncommon, but that day, as we returned, I noticed an especially beautiful bunch that gave me an idea. Without saying anything, I parked the car, called a couple of the black boys, and led them off to where my spray of orchids hung high among the branches. Having located it I told one of the boys to climb up and get it, and under threat of the most awful punishment, not to damage the cluster in the least.

He did as he was told, and in a few minutes I was holding the most magnificent cluster of orchids that one can well imagine. I even counted them, and learned that there were twenty-seven full-blown orchids in that single spray. Then I took it back to camp and presented it to Dot Davison—the largest cluster of orchids, I should imagine, that any lady ever received. But then, I venture to say that orchids were never worn in a more informal manner, for Dot immediately pinned them to her worn and thorn-torn khaki hunting suit.

We had sighted a herd of buffalo on our first aerial scouting trip over the Duma River, and early one morning set off in the hope of photographing them. We had tried half heartedly several times before, but each time they had been out in the open and we had not been able to approach. This time, however, our boys had told us that we could approach them under cover, so we set about the task.

The herds of game were, if anything, thicker than usual that day. We passed through seemingly endless herds of wildebeest, kongoni, and zebra. Impalla and waterbuck were forever about us, and herds of giraffe could be seen in almost every direction. Wart hogs, with their tails up like flag poles, ran along beside us now and then. Grant's and Thompson's gazelles gazed as us with their big bright eyes. Ostriches appeared now and then and mongoose, looking very much like prairie dogs in the grass, darted here and there. Now and then a solemn-looking secretary bird eyed us wisely, or greater and lesser bustard took long runs across the plain before rising clumsily into the air, and about every

FIVE-GALLON BABY. Osa and I trying to coax Toto Tembo into camp a short time after he was captured. The little fellow was quite willing to be friendly and after a few days was the favorite pet of everyone. We had a great deal of trouble getting enough milk as he drank five gallons a day.

MOUNTAIN LEOPARD. A fine example of mountain leopard. The leopard of the plains is the same species as that of the mountains, but for some reason the mountain leopard has darker and richer coloring. A few seconds after this picture was made, he made a leap for the camera. Fortunately he did not reach the aperture where the lenses were protruding from the blind.

clump of trees the ground monkeys played, or baboons barked and chattered.

It was a typical day on the Serengetti Plains, and if ever you want to learn how drab and pitiful and altogether unnatural any circus menagerie really is, just visit this wonderland of game on such a day.

A few miles from camp a lone cheetah bounded across ahead of us. A little farther on several spotted, laughing hyenas were quarreling over the bones of some antelope that had been killed the night before. A mother giraffe nudged her baby, pushing it away from us when we seemed to her sense of precaution to be passing too near.

Through miles of game we drove—none of the animals showing any great signs of fright. They moved aside to let us pass, of course, and at a distance of a couple of hundred yards snorted and stamped to show their disapproval, or stood and watched us mildly as we went on.

The buffalo had been reported along the Duma River, and as we approached it we went more carefully, but though we searched for hours we could not find the herd, and so chose the shade of a magnificent mimosa tree in order to rest and have lunch. The buffalo, we suspected, had withdrawn to parts unknown, and the day was fearfully hot. Consequently, after our lunch of eland sandwiches, partridge breasts, Osa's dried apple pie, and hot tea from our thermos bottles, we dozed until three o'clock or so, and started back for camp.

The game, long before this time, had withdrawn to the

shade of the trees to doze during the heat of the day, but half way back to camp we sighted a cloud of vultures circling slowly about overhead somewhat off our course. We knew from long experience that they were probably waiting for a lion to finish his meal in order that they might have the privilege of taking his leavings. And so it proved.

But the lion was an old one—we could tell by his dark and shaggy mane. Furthermore, he was thin, and no longer the powerful creature he had once been. There he was, in the broiling sun, slowly eating while he kept his eye on those hundreds of waiting scavengers. We could see, from the marks on the ground, that the lion had been pulling the topi he had killed toward the shade of a clump of trees. But the carcass had become wedged among the low thorn bush in a little depression and he could get it no farther.

I started my camera at a considerable distance, and presently we moved closer. He kept his eye on us, but did nothing else, until the second time we moved forward. That, however, he did not approve. He rose to his feet and growled, lashing his tail back and forth as if he might charge. He thought better of it, however, and presently left the dead topi and retreated to the shade sixty or seventy feet away. No sooner had he left his kill, however, than the vultures flocked down upon it and, with a snarl and a series of leaps, the old lion was standing over the topi again, fiercely determined to protect his meal.

Off sailed the vultures, of course, to resume their endless circling, or to perch upon the branches of near-by trees, or stand hideously about on the ground at a safe distance from the angered lion. It is always that way with vultures. They will wait from dawn to dusk in order to appease their horrible appetites, though as dark comes on they always leave. Even then, however, they will return at daybreak if a morsel of meat is to be found.

These unlovely birds are, I believe, quite the greediest creatures that can be imagined. Osa and I have often seen them when they were so gorged with food that they could not fly. This often happens, and it is both ridiculous and a bit revolting to see them running awkwardly along, with their wings spread, trying to take off, and failing time after time. They tire of the effort, finally, of course, and sit gruesomely about waiting for their food to digest before they can take to the air again.

We watched these scavengers of the air for a time as they played their waiting game with the old lion. But the picture was not a pretty one, and we left, finally. Even on the Serengetti Plains there are phases of life that are not entirely pleasant.

Some days later Osa reported having seen a lioness and two very young cubs some miles from camp, and the following morning she and I went out to photograph them. We found them readily, for they had not moved, and instantly we saw that the beautiful young mother had brought her cubs into the world not more than three or four days before. They were so small that they wabbled on their funny feet when they walked. We stopped the car at some distance, in order to let them look us over. But when we moved up, as we did several times, we were eyed with suspicion by the mother. And finally, when we had approached to within about twenty feet, she was obviously perturbed. She, herself, did not give way an inch, but gave a low growl which immediately sent the awkward little fellows back into the bushy donga at the edge of which she stood.

We watched and photographed for some time, and seeing a dead hyena near by, began to wonder if there was not more to this than appeared on the surface.

Here this mother lion was, a good five miles from water, and with two babies that could not, as yet, make a journey of such a distance. And the mother, rather plainly, was both hungry and thirsty. She was sleek enough, but she was somewhat gaunt, and we decided that it was probable that she had had neither food nor water since she had sought out this donga in which to give birth to her cubs. She dared not leave them either, for hyenas—witness the one she had killed—might readily attack the defenseless little fellows in her absence.

Now we had no sooner reached this conclusion than Osa got an idea, so off we went to carry out her plan. We hurried back to camp, cut the top out of a five-gallon petrol tin, took another filled with water, and started back. As we approached the donga Osa shot a zebra, which I made fast with a running loop to the back of the car. And now we drove up to within a safe distance of the lioness, and while Osa stood guard with a gun, I got out, dug a hole, sank the open-topped petrol tin in the ground, packed the earth about it, and filled it from the other tin. I next cast off the rope from the zebra kill, and we drove the car off for a hundred yards, where we stopped and watched the result with our glasses.

We had no sooner left than the lioness got to her feet, sniffed the air, and looked about. Certainly she had smelled the water and the meat, and in another moment she was advancing deliberately toward them. She stopped between the zebra and the water—looked first in one direction and then in the other. It almost seemed as if she could not make up her mind which she wanted most. But finally the water won. She went to the petrol tin and drank. She seemed not to want to quit drinking, and must have taken almost half that five gallons before she turned to her meal. Even then, however, she did not begin to eat at once. Instead, she sank her teeth into the zebra's neck, and backed off toward the donga, pulling the kill as she went.

The last we saw of her was as she disappeared among the bushes, with her two little cubs, which had bobbed up into sight, frisking awkwardly about their mother as the leaves closed about them.

I turned to look at Osa, and found her face wreathed with smiles. She had done her good deed for that day and was completely happy. So I refilled the petrol tin with water from our water bottles and we drove back to camp.

Those two cubs must be almost half-grown lions now.

Such experiences as these are what make visits to the

Serengetti Plains so utterly delightful. I am forever being told that people want to hear stories of terrible danger, of fierce and deadly animals, of battle, murder, and sudden death.

Perhaps they do, but I doubt it. I have seen thrilling doings among the wild life of Africa. I have had my narrow escapes from death, and so has Osa. But in a world already filled with all the difficulties and unpleasantness that our world is, why should people ask to hear of more? I don't believe they really mean it, and I am certain that they, as well as we, would much prefer the beauty of the great game fields as they really are, to the exaggerated stories so often told of fierce and deadly animals, and of mighty hunters forever barely missing sudden and awful death.

There are dangers in Africa, certainly, and anyone who lives among the animals for long enough will encounter them. But animals are considerate, by and large. It is only man who fails in that respect.

6

SINCE our return to America from this series of airplane safaris, I suppose that one question has been asked us much more often than any other, and that question is "How can you live in your airplane when you take long trips away from your base?"

We ourselves wondered how that would work, and before we accepted the planes from the builders we had them incorporate all sorts of ideas that we, with such use in mind, thought would help. "Osa's Ark," the bigger plane of the two (and the one we had had painted with zebra stripes), was originally designed to carry ten people, and was powered with two Wasp super-charged motors. We, of course, never intended to carry that many people at once, and so, in our rearrangement of its ample interior, we had some of the chairs taken out. In their stead we had a soft, leather-upholstered couch built in on one side, while opposite it we installed two chairs which were so designed as to make another couch when they were folded down.

Here, then, were beds for two, but in addition we added every kind of rack that could be devised for our belongings. There were stowage compartments beneath the couch and beneath the chairs. There were baggage compartments for-

127

ward of the pilot's cockpit, and at six points, inside and outside, there were permanently mounted unipods on which, as
we required them, cameras could be mounted. The plane
was also fitted with a lavatory, and after much hunting
about we found an ideal little gasoline stove (two burners
and an oven) which, with a most compact little outfit of
pots and pans, served us perfectly whenever we required
them. Another compact box contained dishes and table ware,
while foodstuffs were packed in other boxes still. Inasmuch
as fish, birds, and game were always easy to obtain, we were
forced to carry only reasonably small supplies of other
foods, consisting mostly of prepared flour and tinned foods.

With such an arrangement, consequently, and with the
supplies that we could readily carry, we were remarkably
free to go and come, or, if we cared to do so (and we did
on many occasions), to land on distant rivers, lakes, or
swamps, or even on the plains among the wild animals,
there to remain for days at a time, often at otherwise impossible distances from our bases of supplies, or in regions not
otherwise open to visits except after long and arduous journeys that would hardly have been possible to us.

It is true that hippo and crocodiles sometimes made water
landings a bit dangerous, and that ant hills, pig holes, rocks,
and soft earth sometimes made landing on the plains a problem. Furthermore, wild animals often insisted on stampeding under us when we were about to land. On one occasion
Vern and I had to fly about for more than long enough at
one of our "homemade" airports before we could land,

A LION COMING FROM HIS CAVE. A beautiful specimen of taffy-maned lion leaving his cave. He wasn't quite awake when this picture was made from the security of a blind. Hearing the noise of the cameras, he came out to investigate and, after a few minutes, was reassured and returned to finish his siesta.

THE SLEEPING ELEPHANT. A fine type of elephant who is just about as large as elephants ever get. We caught him asleep during the middle of the day; it is probable he went to sleep when the shade of the larger tree was over him, but as the sun moved across the sky the shade moved too,

owing to the fact that a herd of zebra had thoughtlessly preëmpted the landing strip.

When Osa, Vern Carstens, Bob Moreno, and I went off "into the blue" with only the big plane for company, Osa and I usually slept in the plane, while Bob and Vern slept under the wing. Sometimes, however, we added a small tent to our luggage, and then Osa and I used that, turning the interior of the plane over to Vern and Bob.

Thus it was simple enough (and certainly comfortable enough) to do more or less as we pleased, except for the problem of petrol supplies and landing fields in rough country. These two problems caused us more than a little work, of course, and only by the most careful possible planning were we able to carry out the innumerable flights that we made. Weeks before we ourselves left America we shipped a large quantity of 87-octane gasoline (which was necessary for our super-charged Wasp motors) out to Nairobi. It left New York in 50-gallon drums, but once it arrived in Nairobi a large part of it was put into five-gallon tins in order to make its transport easier. Then, by motor car and porters, this was distributed throughout the country in places about which we expected to fly—some in the vicinity of Lake Rudolf—some in the Belgian Congo—some down in Tanganyika. And, of course, we kept a supply in Nairobi in order that we might call for it there or order it sent to other points as it was required. This distribution of gasoline was far and away the most troublesome part of our whole series of aerial safaris.

Over African Jungles

As to mechanical difficulties with our planes—there literally were none. The reason for that, of course, is not far to seek. The planes and motors, in the first place, were as nearly perfect as such complicated fabrications can be, and in Vern Carstens we had a pilot and mechanic with an almost uncanny ability to understand, to tune, and to repair his charges. With such a combination, therefore, we had far less trouble than we would have had even with the best of motor cars knocked about and manhandled as they always are on safari.

But now, with Garbatulla, the Tana River and the Serengetti Plains behind us, we were off on an aerial safari to a camp site on the slopes of Mt. Kenya.

This magnificent peak, which rises 17,044 feet above sea level, stands almost on the Equator. It is the more majestic and beautiful, too, for being a lone peak in an otherwise mountainless region. Its mighty and gently swelling base covers an enormous area, and its abrupt and snow-clad peak looks down on such magnificent forest-covered slopes as can hardly be duplicated in the world.

It is, of course, an extinct volcano, and its towering central core is denuded and bare, save for the snow fields and glaciers that cling to it. For so long, however, have its ancient fires been extinguished that every remnant of the former crater has long since vanished, worn away in the course of countless centuries by the wind, the frost and the rains that have been constantly at work. Time was when its massive summit towered still higher than it now does into the African sky, lifting itself for perhaps another two thousand feet above the several steep and denuded pyramids of snow-swept rock that now form so impressive a landmark on its ancient crest.

Except for this rugged apex, however, the mountain is covered with a most magnificent natural growth. Below an altitude of about 10,500 feet, the vast forests lie, and among them abound many of the most interesting animals of Africa. Elephant, buffalo, black rhino, lion, leopard, most of the smaller cats, many kinds of forest antelope, monkeys by the thousand, giant forest hogs, all are to be found upon these forested slopes, and in the streams are to be found such numbers of brown and rainbow trout as might go to make a veritable fisherman's heaven.

Raymond Hook, too, lives on the slopes of this imperial mountain, and inasmuch as Raymond is an old, old friend of ours, who knows this district as no other man, probably, has ever known it, we naturally turned to him for help. He immediately promised, too, to assist us with our task if we would make our camp in the vicinity of his home, which lies in the Nanyuki district. We jumped at the chance, of course, for not only is Raymond himself unique and inval-uable, but his delightful wife is also thoroughly acquainted with the region and the animals, for she, too, has spent most of her life in Africa and loves this beautiful portion of the world. We count the Hooks among our very best friends, and in Mrs. Hook Osa knew that she would have a com-panion of rare understanding.

Consequently, one fine day, Vern, Osa, and I flew up to Nanyuki and landed in a clearing near the grass and log house that is the Hooks' home. We were welcomed royally, of course, and with the Hooks as guides we inspected the surrounding country, looking for a camp site from which our work could most advantageously be carried on. Under their experienced direction we shortly found an ideal spot, too, on the banks of the little Nanyuki River, not too far from the Hooks' home.

Having made our selection, we took off once more for Nairobi, and turned our attention to packing our motor cars with all the endless supplies and equipment that a long stay in a semi-permanent camp would require. Having completed that complicated task, we sent the cars off under the command of Fritz Malewsky, who had joined us at Ngronet, and gave him the "boys" that he would require in setting up camp and in helping Raymond to level off the clearing in which we had landed on our first visit. This was vital to our plan, for we had decided to use the planes as much as possible in photographing Mt. Kenya, and in searching about for other worlds to conquer.

Our party, this time, was to be smaller, for Arthur Sanial had by now returned to America to take up his work where he had dropped it, and Hugh Davis, too, had returned. Thus, when we had given Fritz and Raymond time to prepare for our coming, Osa, Vern, Bob Moreno, and I took off from the Nairobi flying field and winged our way off to our new camp beside the Nanyuki.

AT THE WATERHOLES. During the middle of the day, the game stands around seemingly half asleep, moving about with the shade. Usually they drink but once during the day, but they often stand in the shade for hours before going the few hundred yards to water.

STAGNANT DRINKING WATER. In the waterholes is mostly stagnant, alkaline water that seeps among the reed grass. Often a river with clear, cool water will be near, but the game prefers the more brackish water—probably being afraid of lurking lions or leopards among the thick undergrowth along the stream.

A LAUGHING HYENA. Not all hyenas laugh—only this spotted species. When he does laugh, it is the silliest, craziest sound one can imagine. This fellow does not have the leaf in his mouth as you would at first suppose. He was walking along through the undergrowth when he saw me and stopped with his chin over the protruding leaf.

Over African Jungles

Beautiful as the Kina River camp had been, this new one beside the little stream on the gentle, lower slopes of Mt. Kenya was more so. Our tents were arranged along the stream, not more than twenty or thirty feet from it, and Osa, many and many a time, caught plenty of fish for our meals even when she gave herself only a handful of minutes before they were to be cooked. In most of the pools she would have a strike every time she cast, and while she often caught trout weighing two and three pounds, they were, for the most part, from a half to three quarters of a pound, which, as every fisherman knows, are exactly right for the most particular palate.

The water was cool, too. In fact, it was cold, and I often had to warm it in order to get it to the proper temperature of 65 degrees when I was developing my film. So swift was the stream as well that there were no mosquitoes, and because we were at an elevation of over six thousand feet, the climate was flawless, with magnificently clear days, and nights so cold that we invariably slept under four or five blankets.

Our boys cut firewood from the cedars and pines of the forest about us, and quite often, as we sat about our brisk campfire in the beautiful evenings, the monkeys came to the opposite bank of the stream and watched us, chattering mildly as they sat there.

From the Hooks we got fresh milk and cream, as well as strawberries, corn on the cob, sweet potatoes, beans, and other supplies that usually are not to be had in camp, and

133

altogether we found that this particular section of Africa's tropics was a near approach to absolute perfection. Antelope were all about, too, as well as innumerable game birds. Consequently, with these and our tinned supplies, we were constantly fed on such meals as could not possibly be duplicated at the finest resort hotel in all the world.

Once camp was prepared to suit us in every detail, we cut out a wide lane through the trees and bushes, and thus made a sort of forest boulevard up which, once the planes had landed, we could taxi them from the flying field, in order that they might be kept close beside our tents. One can readily see from this that camping in Africa need not be an experiment filled with hardships.

There were, of course, more reasons than one for our choice of this camp site. Its beauty naturally appealed to us, but, after all, we are practical folks, and our job was to photograph animals. We had had an eye out, therefore, for this, and not far back of the spot that we had chosen lay an area abounding in deep canyons, rocky valleys, and winding dongas, among which were many holes in the rocks, together with occasional black-mouthed caves. And in these varied dens a surprising number of carnivorous animals— cats and cheetahs—made their homes. Consequently we invariably heard, on every night, the sounds of lions, leopards, and other smaller cats.

All of this, of course, intrigued me mightily, and one of the first tasks at which I set the boys, once camp was settled, was the erection of blinds here and there in likely spots, so that I could use them when the animals had come to accept them as part of the local scenery, in my ever-present task of photography. And, as luck would have it, I obtained one of my most interesting pictures from one of these blinds within a week of our arrival. It came about when one of the boys reported having seen a lion not far from a cave near which we had built a compact blind several days before, and it was in the very earliest light of the next dawn that Osa, Fritz, Bob Moreno and I made our way to the blind, carefully set up our sound equipment, and crept inside in the hope that the lion, or at least something, would show up.

An hour passed, I suppose, with nothing whatever save the cave mouth visible to us. Off in the distance the monkeys were chattering in the trees. Birds overhead in the tall trees sang or squawked or scolded. From an opening some distance down the slope came the trampling of heavy feet as some ugly-tempered rhino charged a few steps in futile search of some half-imaginary enemy. But there ahead of us the cave mouth stood silent and deserted. It began to look to me as if the morning would be wasted—that we should have remained at camp, or have gone out to photograph a herd of buffalo about which Raymond had told us on the preceding evening.

I was half dreaming over all this, and paying no attention whatever to what might be happening at the entrance to the cave, when I felt Osa's hand touch me lightly on the knee.

Over African Jungles

I glanced up at once, and there, not more than twenty feet away, stood a lion. He was almost squarely in front of us, but I was so surprised at his ability to appear in that fashion without a sound that for once I almost forgot to turn the switch and start the camera. However, I came to myself promptly enough and snapped the switch. He stopped for a moment as he heard the machine, glanced casually around, and, as if quite unconscious of our presence, continued his leisurely and somewhat aimless advance toward the cave.

He had, undoubtedly, fed well the night before, and now, heavy with food, was quite willing to sleep off the effects. He was one of the handsomest lions I ever saw, I really believe, and he was big, too—big enough to be able to care for himself very well indeed, if necessary, against any animal in all the country around. His hair was light colored and curly, which is very unusual, and I can't think of a better way to describe him than to quote Osa.

"Why, Martin," she whispered, still with her hand on my knee, "he's a perfectly beautiful platinum blond."

Elephants, buffalo, and rhino, of course, such a lion would not trouble. He would not be likely ever even to cross the path of a hippo or a crocodile. But anything else in all the region, save man, of course, would be quite willing to give way to this somewhat casual and full-bellied lion as he looked about for a place in which to take a nap.

I was tending the camera now, and watching carefully. He stopped and looked about. Certainly he showed no

HUNTING PARTY. Masai warriors on the Serengetti Plains. These hunting parties leave their manyettas for a trip of several weeks, hunting honey, skins, wildebeest tails for ornaments, lion manes for head-dresses, and a certain amount of dried antelope. Then they return to their tribal home boasting of the brave acts they performed while they were away.

YOUNG RENDILLE GIRL. This girl was of more than usual interest to us, because about eight years ago, when she was a child of eight or nine, we had photographed her while she was tending a small flock of goats. Osa had caught and held her while I made the picture. She had cried and tried to run away. She remembered the incident and laughed about it.

familiarity with the cave before which he was standing. It seemed to me that he would act quite differently if it were his den. Nevertheless, he moved on toward it, and I gave up doubting as he turned to enter.

All of this, up to now, had been very quiet and orderly, and I was expecting to stop the camera in another moment, for he was half way into the cave, when suddenly, and without the slightest warning, he let out a muffled snarl. He recoiled for a moment, his muscles tense, roared, leaped back, his teeth bared, and in another instant bolted away among the rocks and trees. He had come up quite casually and noiselessly. He had departed in a flurry of roars and leaps. But what, in the name of Heaven, could make a full-grown and thoroughly capable lion depart in any such undignified fashion?

I was leaning forward now, my eyes intent upon the cave mouth, while still I kept the camera trained upon it. I had no wish to miss a single second if whatever had frightened the lion should appear. What it could be I could not imagine. Nothing that lives in any African cave is a lion's equal. Yet this something must be, for there was no doubt about the abruptness of that lion's retreat.

I thought I heard a faint sound from the cave. In a moment I was sure I heard it—a small sound. But what it was I could not make out. I watched steadily, and suddenly I saw a tuft of fur. And then, to my utter amazement, four tiny little baby cheetahs appeared at the cave mouth. They could hardly have been more than a few days old, and their little eyes blinked in the sunlight that seemed too bright for them. I let the camera run for another minute or so. One of the little fellows yawned prodigiously and another stumbled over his own feet, while Osa, quiet until now, could hold in no longer, and off, somewhere, up the rocky gorge into which he had disappeared, the lion let out one last and futile roar.

"What sweet little things," Osa remarked at last.

"Humph," I grunted, stopping the machine. "I suppose you want 'em."

"Of course I do!"

"You'll have to feed 'em from a bottle."

"Of course," she agreed. "But we have plenty of bottles, and I brought nipples especially."

And so, to go with the first five hundred feet of film that we exposed there on the slopes of Kenya, we packed four furry little cheetah babies back to camp, to join with Wah, our gibbon ape, with Rikki and Tikki, our two mongooses, and with other creatures that came, from time to time, into our hands.

But it must not be supposed that wild animal photography is always so simple as this incident might lead one to imagine. One does not usually merely pick up his camera and wander out to photograph some obliging beast that goes through his part like a Hollywood extra. As a matter of general rule, animals almost never do as you want them to, or stay where you would prefer to have them stay. Still, we have had long years of experience in Africa, and have learned more than a little of the best way to handle each species of game.

The wind, of course, must be from the animal to us. The sun's rays must be from behind and on the animal. Again, it is never well to have the horizon or the sky in the picture, for the result will be flat, and halation, that bane of photographers, is apt to ruin an otherwise good photograph. And heat waves, of course, make photography almost impossible.

With all of these points, and others still, in mind, Osa and I always try to "out guess" the animals, and try to determine in advance what they might do, or where they might go. It is not too often that good pictures are made by seeing the animal first and setting one's camera up afterward. The best method is to set up the camera at a place before which the animal is likely to appear, in order to have everything in perfect order if he does appear.

It was for this reason that, having found the caves not far from camp, we built our blinds at the most advantageous points, left them for a time so that the animals would get accustomed to their presence, and then used them, from time to time, as our experience dictated. Many, many times, of course, we were fooled, and the animals failed entirely to appear, or appeared beyond the range of our cameras or in places in which they could not, for other reasons, be photographed.

But naturally, too, we searched farther afield for other points at which to build blinds, and finally located an extraordinary V-shaped cleft in the side of a little canyon, at the apex of which a likely looking cave curved darkly away into the rocks. The sides of this V were fifty feet or so in height, and were almost vertical as well. These walls were composed of earth, clay, and rocks to which more or less vegetation clung, but up which no animal—unless it were a monkey—could possibly have made its way. Furthermore, the cave could not be approached save by the open mouth of the V, and, leaving plenty of room on each side, we built our blind directly in the center of this opening. Immediately before the cave Bob arranged three rocks, between which, and well protected by them, he placed the microphone of our sound equipment. Then, in a shallow trench that led to the blind, we ran the wire, and when it was all arranged to Bob's satisfaction, we covered the wire with earth and leaves, leaving very little to tell that we had wired the place for sound. And, too, because there was plenty of space, we erected a blind amply large for two movie cameras and one still camera. Then, knowing that we might have to swing the cameras well to the right and left, we left an unusually large opening. We never thought of the danger that such construction might place us in, for animals usually try to get away from anything they do not understand, and because of our thoughtlessness in this case we were very unexpectedly placed in one of the most dangerous situations that we have ever experienced.

We left this new blind alone for a few days, and finally, early one morning, Osa, Bob, Raymond Hook, and I made our way to it, set up our cameras, connected our sound equipment to the buried wire, climbed into the blind, and began our watch.

Nothing much happened for a time. A few little animals appeared stealthily among the grass and shrubs. A crow flew past and, settling in a tree near by, talked in his guttural voice for an hour or so. We heard little scurryings and squeakings from beneath the grass, and could make out the distant chattering of monkeys in the trees farther down the canyon. But suddenly there was a tiny sound of hurrying little creatures in the grass before the blind, and a fine, full-grown female leopard appeared. She stealthily entered the V at our left, smelled the bushes here and there, approached the cave, started into it, turned back, and all through this she stopped now and then, pointing like a setter dog. Her ears would go back. Her tail would lash from side to side, and at every sound of the wind in the trees or of a bird overhead she would stop and look about. She seemed all nerves, as though suspecting something wrong. It is not unlikely, of course, that she faintly got our scent, or possibly the microphone and the buried wire told her sensitive nose that all was not as it should have been.

Still, despite her nervousness, she was an ideal subject, and the camera had long since been started. The result was that I filmed every movement that leopard made for nearly half an hour. Several times she started to enter the cave, but changed her mind each time, to our great disappointment. We wanted her to go in, whereupon Raymond, who was standing almost directly behind me, was to fire his gun through the roof of the blind. That, we thought, would frighten her, and we would get some real action as she came dashing out. Furthermore, we wanted her to make some noise, for while I was getting excellent pictures she was absolutely noiseless in her motions, and the sound apparatus was getting nothing.

We had, I suppose, grown more or less blasé about her, for she had been out there in front of us for an unusual length of time, when suddenly she turned directly toward the blind and saw me as I made some movement in tending my camera. In a flash she made two or three powerful leaps toward us. Before I realized what was happening she sprang squarely through the too large opening in the blind, and struck the camera behind which I was standing, sending it back against my face. That in itself half stunned me, but then, with such a crash in my right ear as made me think that the sky had fallen, Raymond's gun exploded in her very eyes. She was clutching at the camera not eighteen inches from me, and suddenly I felt her hot blood splash across my cheek. I still was too astounded to realize just what had happened, but then I saw her hold on the camera relax, and in another moment she fell limp, her head and body dangling down among the legs of the tripod of the camera she had struck, her hind legs supported by the lower edge of the opening in the blind.

So quickly had she come that I had done literally nothing whatever. But Raymond, collected and accurate as he always seems to be, had fired past my ear, and with that one quick shot had sent his bullet squarely into the ferocious cat's brain. I thanked my lucky stars for Raymond, you can be sure, and even after it was all over I felt decidedly shaky and unnerved.

Oddly enough, though we had been very successful up to the time of this event with daylight photography from the blinds, we seemed, from then on, to have no luck at all. That I had been badly shaken by having the leopard come at me so fiercely I realize perfectly, and it is not to be doubted that Osa, Bob, and Raymond were similarly effected. Whether that had any effect on our later luck I do not know. I do not see why such a result would follow logically, and yet I cannot help wondering.

With bad luck the rule for several days we decided to break into our photographic routine, in order to relieve ourselves of the monotony of failure. It may be, too, that we all had some subconscious desire to break the "jinx," as well. At any rate, we decided to make a flight concerning which we had often talked—a flight over the peak of Mt. Kenya, which towered for more than two miles above our camp, and well over three above sea level.

We seized the first opportunity, therefore, when the snow-covered peak was free of clouds, and early on as beautiful a day as one could possibly imagine, we took off from the clearing, and soared away through the clear air, intent on looking down on Mt. Kenya from above, and of photographing this gorgeous giant of Kenya Colony.

We climbed for seven or eight thousand feet with the

utmost ease, but, because of the fact that our flying field lay at an elevation of about six thousand, we now were about fourteen thousand feet above sea level, and the going became more difficult. Only the fact that our motors were super-charged made it possible for us to continue to rise at all, for our plane was never built to break any altitude records, and its great weight could be urged upward only with almost painful effort.

Still we kept at it, and little by little we climbed until the snow fields, the glaciers, and the steep, bare peaks were there, just beyond our windows.

Ten thousand times we had looked up at the crest of this gigantic mountain from the plains and hills below. For years we had been familiar with its ever-changing moods. And always we had admired its amazing beauty. But now, with those all but insurmountable crags close beside us, we obtained a new and still more marvelous view of this snow-clad giant of the Equator.

Up and up we climbed, passing the very highest peak. Our motors, under Vern's expert guidance, slowly raised the plane until full two thousand feet below us the crest thrust itself sharply up.

Never have I seen a sight so beautiful. Throughout the whole blue sky not even a faint shred of cloud was visible. Below us the rocks and snows and glaciers stood. Further down lay the zone of lobelias and grass. Still further down bamboo ringed the mountain 'round, and on below that the almost endless forests stretched on down the slope, billow-

BABOONS IN FLIGHT. Baboons fleeing across a small river. They were not much afraid of the water; they seemed to enjoy it. Usually they selected a place where there were rocks in the stream but these rocks were slippery and they would generally slip off, then continue their flight by swimming.

SHADOWS ON THE CLOUDS. An interesting shadow effect on the clouds, a mile above the ground, with the shadow of the big plane near the shadow of the small plane from which I was

ing over hills, sweeping away through valleys until, at last, they met the plains that continued on to a horizon so distant as to seem impossible.

I had taken up an Eyemo camera as soon as the view gave me an opportunity to photograph to good advantage, and constantly, throughout the flight, I kept it up. But an Eyemo carries only one hundred feet of film, and, in addition, the spring that drives it must be rewound each time it has driven thirty-five feet of film past the lens.

Now theretofore, I had never considered the winding of an Eyemo spring as a task of any consequence whatever. But as we climbed higher and higher into the rarefied air about that enormous peak, my strength seemed to fail me almost utterly, and I labored and panted over that simple task in the most discouraging manner. It was bitterly cold, as well, as I leaned out the window at the side of the co-pilot's seat, and what with winding the camera spring, changing color filters, passing my camera to Osa or Bob in exchange for another each time a hundred feet of film had been exposed, I grew almost exhausted, and became so weak that I could hardly bring myself to continue.

We passed over chasms in which the snow lay a hundred feet in depth. Frozen lakes were here and there in depressions. Then Osa picked out the exact spot to which she and I had climbed eight years before, and pointed out the place at which we had made the camp in which she had come down with double pneumonia. We had known then how serious our situation had been, but as we looked at that exposed spot from the security of our plane, I wondered how it was that she had ever come out of that experience alive.

We had been away from camp for five hours before I had used up all my supply of film. And it was only then that I told Vern to start down. And now, in thirty minutes from the biting cold of nineteen thousand feet, we landed on our flying field again, close beside the forest where, for unnumbered generations, the local natives of the region had known the snow and ice of the vast peak that stood above them only as they knew the legends of their tribes. And overheated as our camp now seemed, it took us all of two hours before we could shiver away the last of the chill that the thin air above Mt. Kenya had given us. And all of us, undoubtedly because of the rapidity of our descent, felt "jittery" for an equal length of time.

We tried our hand again at the blinds we had set up, but our "jinx" held good, and so, at Raymond Hook's suggestion, we decided to make a long trek through the forest to a clearing that lay far up the mountainside at an elevation of about eleven thousand feet. Here, Raymond assured us, was the place for animals, for, in the clearing, lay a salt lick to which the animals from all that side of Mt. Kenya often came.

Our party was quite impressive as we started out, for Raymond brought pack horses and pack mules, in addition to a number of his native boys. All these, together with our boys, made quite a showing. Our party, too, added to the number, for while Vern and Bob had decided on a little safari of their own and so did not accompany us, both Raymond and Mrs. Hook did, and Fritz Malewsky as well. Thus Osa and I were a part of such a group as rarely goes with us, and we looked forward with more than a little pleasure to the trip.

Leaving camp in the early morning, we safaried all day through the forest, crossing swift little trout streams from which it was difficult to drag Osa, following along trails where the fresh spoors of rhino and buffalo were plain, where elephant tracks showed here and there, and where, overhead, the monkeys and the birds made an endless show.

It was late in the afternoon when we chose a place for camp under a beautiful, spreading tree not far from a stream. The salt lick lay not far off, and while camp was being set up, Raymond and I went off to inspect it, while Osa and Mrs. Hook went fishing.

The salt lick offered excellent opportunities for pictures, and having decided on the best methods to pursue, Raymond and I returned to camp to find the freshly caught trout already sizzling in the pan. What a dinner that was, in the clear, bracing air there on the side of Mt. Kenya, and how thoroughly we enjoyed that evening about the campfire, listening to the stories that Raymond and Mrs. Hook told us of their years of adventure in the forest.

We went to bed early, and were awakened at dawn by the boys who told us that a rhino was at the salt lick. We dressed hurriedly, of course, picked up our cameras and guns, and with Raymond and me leading, while the others

147

followed at some distance so as to watch without running the risk of frightening the rhino, we headed toward the clearing.

We were hardly well under way, however, when the rhino decided to leave. We followed him until he entered the forest, and then we lost sight or him, though we could hear him feeding. Consequently I set up my cameras, hoping that he would return, for only in the opening would it be possible to obtain any pictures.

Osa and the others now came up, and as they did so a herd of buffalo dashed out of the bush, scattering in every direction as they crossed the clearing. All our guns went up as a matter of course, but the buffalo disappeared into the bush again, while our rhino, excited, no doubt, by the galloping buffalo, burst into the open and dashed away.

One of the porters, however, who had been left at a little distance, appeared presently, and told us of another rhino that was in the bushes a few hundred yards away. We quietly gathered up our cameras, of course, but the wind was wrong, and we were forced to make a roundabout detour. We entered the bush, finally, and after a careful advance, set up our cameras while Osa went forward, for the ground was fairly open, and took up her position while I started the camera. The sound of the camera, or possibly the breaking of a twig or some other sound, startled the rhino almost immediately, and all in a moment his tail was up and he was bearing down upon Osa with all the determination of a locomotive. She raised her gun, but, though I fully expected

A FISHERMAN'S PARADISE. Osa would rather fish than do anything else, and Africa offered all the fishing one could wish. Rainbow and brown trout in the clear mountain streams; bass in the lakes; and catfish in the sluggish streams. As the natives seldom fish, every stretch of water is a fisherman's paradise.

THE SMALLEST BABOON. Mickey Mouse, we named him, this smallest baboon of the colony that we lived beside for so many weeks. He was always a source of amusement and, much to his mother's annoyance, he was a natural born explorer. She was constantly worried for fear he'd wander away and get into trouble or be lost.

her to fire, she did not. The rhino was close, now, and I almost shouted to her, when suddenly the old fellow changed his direction and went crashing away until he was lost to sight. And there, we felt, was proof that *that* rhino, at least, had acted as we had supposed he would. But then, Osa had had her full share of nerve to wait, for he had turned off when he was not more than twenty feet or so from her. It is not everyone, I am sure, who would have waited until he had come so close.

For a week we remained at our camp near the salt lick, seeing game every day, getting a few pictures, and altogether having a gorgeous time. But time was pressing, and we were forced to return to the Nanyuki camp.

Then, in the next few weeks, we flew over to Mt. Kenya twice, and on one of these flights found the summit wreathed in clouds while a snowstorm eddied its stinging flakes all about the sullen peaks. We made other flights, as well, and on a number of occasions flew over the forest. Several times, while we were in the air, we saw elephants and buffalo in the clearings below, and on one occasion we rented a Puss Moth plane in Nairobi, and from it we made motion pictures of our own two planes in the air.

We acquired more pets, too, for it is a constant temptation to purchase young animals from the natives when they bring the appealing things to camp. It was thus that we obtained a young hyena and a young leopard—an odd assortment, I must admit. And, more odd still, it seemed no time at all before they were both so tame that they had the run of camp.

For three full months we remained there on the slope of Mt. Kenya, and in that time Osa, I really believe, had all the fishing she wanted.

Because our flying field was so convenient, we used our planes constantly; and usually, when we took off, we took two or three of our best black boys with us. They always went, of course, when they were told, but never did they come to the point where they enjoyed it. On the contrary, they were always afraid, and held onto their safety belts grimly. Nor would they more than glance from the windows.

On one occasion I decided to have a talk with several of them about this attitude of theirs, in the hope that I could teach them to relax and enjoy the flights. But, to my surprise, one of the most intelligent of the lot came forth with a remark that I have never forgotten.

"Bwana," he said, "I have been with you for nearly fifteen years. First we walked, and that was fun. Then you brought motor cars, and you know that many, many times those engines stopped and we had to fix them so they would go again.

"Now I know that these indagis go up in the air because the engines make them go. And I know that sometime, when we get up in the air about two miles, the engines are going to stop."

He paused and looked at me seriously.

"And then," he asked, "what are we going to do?"

It was this same fellow, by the way, to whom, one day, I insistently presented a cake of soap.

"For heaven's sake," I remarked, "go take a bath. You smell something awful."

He took the cake of soap meekly enough and turned to go, but thinking of something, he paused.

"Bwana," he said, "would you mind if I told you something?"

"No," I grumbled. "Go ahead."

"Well, bwana," he began, "the white man often tells us black men that we smell. But do you know that to us black people the white man smells every bit as bad as the black man does to you?"

I have thought of that since, and many times I have seen natives go through herds of animals without frightening them to any degree whatever. And I have sometimes approached the same herds when I know that it was only my scent that they detected. And wonder of wonders! They have scattered to the winds. Perhaps the black man's idea on the same subject was not so far wrong after all.

But our three months at Nanyuki, like every other good thing in this world, came to an end at last. We had talked with Raymond about a new region in which he swore the game was endless, and with such a prospect, even Nanyuki could not hold us.

We broke camp, therefore, but we will always remember

those months at Nanyuki where, with Raymond and Mrs. Hook for neighbors, we fished and flew and photographed in one of this world's most delightfully beautiful regions. This region, certainly, as Carl Akeley often said, is "brightest" Africa.

SOMALI GIRLS BATHING. Two girls were surprised while taking a bath in the Tana River. They were not embarrassed. In fact, they thought it was a joke and went ahead bathing. Afterwards they nonchalantly stepped out of the water, donned their robes, and walked away.

TWO FINE FELLOWS. Two baboons who had grown used to our presence and who were always curious about our movements. Baboons often seem mangy, but this particular colony was in the best of health, with thick long hair. At times they chattered as though they wanted to talk to us.

7

WE NOW felt that we had obtained what we needed from the eastern and southern slopes of Mt. Kenya, and that we had better move on. To the west and southwest we could look down from our camp and see hundreds of square miles of plains, thorn bush country, hills, and, in the very far distance, mountains—an alluring country, and we knew from the little we had seen of it in the past that it was good game country. We talked it over with Raymond Hook, consequently, and decided to investigate a certain section of it from the air.

Accordingly Vern gassed up "Osa's Ark" to capacity, and early one clear morning we put off—Vern, Osa and I, together with Mr. and Mrs. Hook.

After an hour Raymond told us that we were entering the country he knew as good game country from safaris he had made years ago. So Vern allowed the ship to settle to within five hundred feet of the ground and immediately we frightened a big herd of buffalo that milled around a little and then settled into a compact group with their heads all facing out, as though in battle formation. A minute later we saw a rhino and her baby. Next we flew over a herd of a hundred or so giraffe—then water buck, ostrich, zebra and

153

all the common game. A flock of vultures arose from their kill—another rhino appeared, and then another. By now we were over the headwaters of the Guaso Nyiro River and a couple of elephants scurried away with their tails up and their big ears flapping. We all got a laugh as they tried to cross a dry, sandy river bed and nearly bogged down. They had started to cross on the run, but were forced to slow down, and in the middle they barely moved as their feet sank deeper and deeper, but they got across all right. Following down the river for an hour we saw very little game, but then we came out over the Kaisoot Desert and found large numbers of animals, though they all stayed near the river. It is strange how the game love the dry desert country. We were forced to gain altitude in order to fly over the Mathews Range. After that we flew over a long table-top mountain where we swooped down to within two hundred feet of the tree tops and saw a rhino, several elephants and a herd of buffalo, although this mountain was at least two or three thousand feet above the desert below. Green vegetation proved that there was water there, but it was a strange place in which to find big game. As we left it, Osa and I resolved that some day we would return, in order to climb this mountain and study the animals.

Then, after five hours in the air, we returned to camp, our minds made up. We would move into the thorn bush country, where we had seen so much game, and try our hands at photographing it.

This thorn bush country is a varied region. There are

open plains and patches of forest, waterholes, rugged hills, caves, and park-like stretches in which, if one is fortunate, as we were, one is likely to find an amazing variety of Africa's most interesting animals.

For the most part, though, the country is flat and is covered with millions upon millions of small thorn bushes. The ground beneath them is soft and seemingly a mixture of sand and earth. Hard, jagged stones are everywhere half buried in the soil, making it uncomfortable for walking, while every thorn bush is the home of thousands of ants. These pestiferous insects live in the pods at the base of each thorn, and as this district contains hundreds of square miles, together with literally millions of thorn bushes, and as each bush is the home of thousands of ants, it can clearly be seen that there are really no conceivable figures enormous enough to cover the probable number of ants. Osa still insists that there are more living creatures in this district than in any similar area on earth, and I certainly do not argue the point with her. An individual ant is nothing to worry about, but in this country they were forever present by the million, and every ant, or so it seemed, picked on us. They got down our backs, into our clothing, our hair—and how they could bite! Oddly enough, they did not seem to bother the natives or the animals, but they certainly made life miserable for us.

I have sometimes said that this is the country of the Lumbwa, though that is not strictly accurate. It is, instead, a sort of no-man's land. On all sides live the Meru, the

Lumbwa, the Nandi, and the Kikuyu, so that in this district may be seen wandering groups from any of these tribes, but the Lumbwa are most numerous because, being a hunting people, they find this country more suited to their needs, and near some of the waterholes they have built a few manyettas where they live during the dry seasons with their cattle, though, when the rains come, they generally push back into their own country again. And the Lumbwa are, to my mind, one of the finest-looking tribes that is to be found in Kenya Colony, and in addition they are brave to the point of fearlessness when it comes to spearing lions and rhinos, and almost any other animals, with their handsome, long-pointed spears.

It was with regret that we broke our Nanyuki camp. We had spent three happy months here—months of freedom and thrills, but all good things must come to an end.

Osa and I wished further to test our theory about rhino, and Raymond Hook insisted that he knew the best rhino district in the northern Kenya country. Osa and I knew the Guaso Nyiro River, for through many years we had explored almost its entire length, but we had never visited its headwaters. Still, we knew it should be fine game country, and we knew that Raymond Hook knew his animals, for he has spent most of his life among them. Then again, Raymond had never been in sympathy with game slaughterers, and we knew he had safaried through thousands of miles of this northern country. Any district he recommended was bound to be good.

Over African Jungles

So Bob and Vern flew back to Nairobi. All the motor cars, save two, were packed with our camping equipment and they, too, returned to Nairobi, leaving only one tent and a few boys to take care of our pet animals. Then we started off to the north with Raymond Hook and Fritz Malewsky, though Osa insisted that Wah and our four baby cheetahs must go with us.

It was a beautiful day, the going was good but slightly muddy, and just at noon we stopped for lunch at a green-scummed waterhole, about which were innumerable tracks of wild animals, including many tracks of rhino. This water was not good enough for us to drink, but about three miles away we could see the outlines of the Guaso Nyiro River, and knew we would have no trouble in getting good, fresh water every day. We did not wish to camp on the river as Raymond felt sure that the rhino country started at this waterhole and we consequently wanted to remain near by.

On the next day we explored the district and found that it lived up to Raymond's description in every way. We saw rhino galore, but made no attempt to photograph them, for we wanted to get the lay of the land first. We saw signs of elephants, as well, while giraffe were about in great numbers, and we saw more impalla than we had ever seen in any other part of Africa. There were signs of buffalo, as well, and we were pleased to find that Orangi, our headman, knew the country thoroughly, although he had not told us so when we were making our plans. I think it probable that he had not known just where we had planned to go.

That day, unfortunately, Raymond developed a bad leg that gave him considerable trouble, and on the next day it was worse, but he said little about it. We went out to get pictures, consequently, and during the day we saw twelve different rhino, and they were quite nice rhino, too—if a rhino can be called nice. We made some good pictures, and Raymond proved what a good shot he was by shooting one in the horn—it was a half-grown rhino that charged when I was not ready for him. It was a case of either shooting him, or discouraging his charge, so Raymond placed a well-aimed bullet about three inches from the tip of his horn. The rhino stopped so suddenly that he rolled over, but quickly was on his feet again and with a sudden whirl was off for parts unknown.

That night Raymond's leg was worse, and on the next morning he decided to return to Nanyuki where he could give it proper care. This left only Osa, Fritz and me to carry on, which we were determined to do, for we knew the lay of the land and its possibilities. We were sorry, however, to have Raymond leave us.

Orangi had long since learned quite a bit about photography and the subjects that we wanted, so we were very much interested when he told us of a waterhole in a dry, rocky river bed near by—one beside which he had camped some years before. We set out on an inspection tour, consequently, resolving to leave the rhino alone for a few days.

The waterhole to which Orangi took us was really not a

waterhole as we knew them up in the desert country, but was, instead, a dry and sandy river bed.

These dry river beds are among the most interesting waterholes in Africa. They never contain surface water except for a few hours after rains, but the water is always there a few feet below the sand, especially at bends of the river where, far below, solid rock or some other formation holds water for long periods. Animals smell the water and dig in the sand with their feet. The water then comes seeping through, though it is strange that the animals know just where to dig. Sometimes there are stretches for miles up and down the river where there is no water and where the animals never attempt to find it.

On either side of the sandy river bed, at the spot to which Orangi took us, were terraces of stone extending about thirty feet above the sand. They were arranged like stairs with each step about six feet above the one below, and the whole formation gave us the impression that thousands of years of rushing waters had worn them that way. Several well-worn trails led down through the rocks to the sand, and these had undoubtedly been used by countless generations of animals coming to drink.

We selected a spot on top of the rocks, at a point away from any of the trails, cut some thorn bush with which partially to conceal ourselves, and then returned to camp, for I had some developing to do.

Just at sunset we went back to the waterhole—Osa, Fritz and I. It was all of an hour, I suppose, before the first animal appeared, and even then it was only a jackal. Dusk had come, but the moon would not rise for another hour, with the result that, as darkness came down, the river bed and its surroundings became less and less distinct until, at last, it was only faintly visible, while the animals that we could make out were usually only darker shadows in the darkness. Often we could only guess what they were from the way they moved.

Off in the distance we could hear various animal sounds from time to time. Faintly the half-insane laughter of hyenas drifted to us on the breeze. An ostrich boomed from behind a patch of thorn bush that lay some distance beyond the waterhole, and reminded us of our first safari when we took exactly such a sound to be the grunt of a lion. It had taken us some time to learn that so impressive a sound could come from the attenuated throat of an ostrich, and even now we sometimes fail to tell the difference. From an opening some distance off came the rattle of hoofs, as if a herd of antelope or zebra had caught a lion's scent, and were stampeding. But suddenly our attention was distracted from such distant sounds when we saw the huge, black shadow of an elephant, just as the great yellow full moon appeared above the horizon.

It is extraordinary how quietly these great beasts can move. Here was an animal weighing two or three tons, perhaps, approaching the waterhole without the slightest sound that we could detect. He came directly toward it, paying not the slightest attention to two or three jackals that scam-

IZZIAH, OUR ELEPHANT GUIDE. Osa demonstrated an Eveready flashlight to our elephant guide Izziah. We gave him the name because we could not pronounce his. He was always interested in everything but the airplanes; he would have nothing to do with them.

OLD JOHN, THE LEADER. Old John, we named him. He seemed to be the leader of the baboon colony, settling all disputes, barking orders to the others, always on the lookout. He must have been a little childish, however, for he would sit for hours chattering and talking to himself.

pered away at his approach, and, reaching the river bed almost beneath us, he curled his trunk and, using it almost like an enormous spoon, he started throwing sand from a little depression where other animals had dug the night before. For ten or fifteen minutes he steadily threw out the sand without a pause. He went at the job in such a business-like way that we felt sure he had dug at that same place time after time, and, in fifteen minutes or so, he had dug so deep that he was forced to get down on his knees to reach the bottom. Then in that awkward position, he seemed to rest, but I am sure he knew what he was doing, for after resting a few minutes he again inserted his trunk and we could hear him sipping water, though the first few sips were evidently filled with sand, for he blew it out. He must have busied himself there for another fifteen minutes, while we on the ledge were watching through our binoculars.

The light was getting better, now, and it was obvious that this first visitor of consequence was a young bull, but while he was still drinking a cow appeared a hundred yards or so away. She was at least as large as the young bull, and she was accompanied by a very tiny little baby, which trotted along so close beside her that at first we failed to see the little fellow at all.

The newcomer approached the pool as directly as the young bull had, but saw, apparently, that he was kneeling in the one place from which water could most easily be obtained. Furthermore, the bull made no move to step aside. Instead, he kept his place, his hind quarters high in the air, his trunk out of sight in the shadow of the pool itself, as if he considered the place entirely his.

For a moment the cow moved about doubtfully, searching, apparently, for a way to reach the water. That she was not satisfied was obvious, but the result was surprising. She complained, in a gentle sort of sound, at the bull's selfishness, but obtaining no results, she suddenly shoved her calf out of harm's way, coiled up her trunk, and with a grunt and a rush, butted the bull powerfully from the rear. There was a squeal and a terrific splash, and I would have given a great deal for a photograph of what happened—which, of course, I could not take, for we had not come prepared to take flashlight pictures. We could not even see clearly just what happened, for no sooner had the incensed cow collided with the bull than he tumbled squarely into the pool, which he almost filled. Water splashed. The young bull squealed, struggled to his feet and slipped once or twice before finally getting out onto the sand. We wondered what would happen next, but that show was over. Without the slightest attempt to defend himself the bull disappeared into the night at a kind of shuffling run, and the cow, carefully keeping her baby from the edge of the pool, cleaned out the sand that had slid into the water, drank her fill, and quietly went off into the darkness, still with her baby almost hidden beside her own black bulk.

For a time the waterhole was deserted again, and then, quite suddenly, the jackals reappeared. A lone bull eland followed, drinking quickly and departing, as if he realized that he must give others a turn, or, more probably, as if he knew that lions and leopards might appear at any time.

And now, from off in the distance, we heard a sound that told us plainly that a rhino was approaching. We could not see the beast, but we could hear him. He would sniff once or twice and advance a way. Then, after a pause, he would snort and we could hear him as he trotted aimlessly about in a circle. And for all of fifteen minutes he kept this up before we could make him out at all. The moon, however, was by now well above the eastern hills, and finally, as it slid still higher, we could make the old fellow out, a good hundred yards away, snorting, trotting about, stopping, sniffing.

For nearly an hour he kept that up, gradually coming closer to the pool as he did so. I have seen the same sort of thing happen before, but never to quite such an extent. Perhaps the mingled scents that reached him from the vicinity of the pool caused him to act as he did. At any rate, he certainly must have trotted about for half a mile or more before he covered the hundred yards to the pool.

But now we could see him clearly. He was within ten yards, perhaps, of the pool, and his investigation seemed largely over, when he let out a prodigious snort, turned quickly about, and there about a hundred yards away, we saw a female rhino with a baby as she appeared from behind some rocks.

The big fellow's snort caused her to reply in kind. Up went his tail, as if it were the flag on a battleship. Up went hers. Another snort. Another reply. And suddenly, with their heads down, each beast broke into a charge. What an opportunity for a camera to miss!

The hundred yards that separated them dwindled to fifty —to forty—to thirty. Certainly, the collision would be enormous, for despite their apparent awkwardness, rhinos can move with surprising speed.

Twenty yards—ten! But suddenly they both stopped, sniffed the air mildly, turned about as if nothing in the world had ever disturbed their equanimity, and then, the big fellow first, and the mother and baby afterward, they approached the waterhole almost nonchalantly, drank what they desired, and disappeared.

The jackals reappeared—several of them—nervously approaching the pool, lapping hurriedly and scurrying away. A hyena followed, stealthily. The jackals stood back and gave him the right of way, but they all disappeared as if by magic when, from up across the valley, came the reverberating roar of a lion that had fed.

Here was one beast that knew his own strength. He might not come soon, for the roar had come from all of a quarter of a mile away. Still, whenever he wished he would come, and would come directly and without fear. One cannot but admire a lion.

And, twenty minutes or so later, he did come—a fine big fellow, still with the bloody marks of his meal upon his face. He came deliberately—majestically, pausing now and then and looking calmly about before moving on. He

TURKANA HEAD-DRESS. A typical Turkana type, wearing the hair
of his ancestors. This man inherited most of his hair from his father;
his eldest son in turn will inherit his. And so on down the ages. It is
matted and kept together with clay.

A YOUNG FEMALE LEOPARD. Photographed from the interior of a blind. There's no doubt in our minds that the leopard is the most beautiful and graceful animal in the world and, like most animals, when undisturbed, does not have the ferocious expression commonly associated with wild animals.

reached the edge of the pool, stood there for a moment, looked about, and dropping down, drank his fill, before moving off and disappearing among the rocks beyond the pool from us.

The moon was almost overhead by now, and we could see clearly, save in the heavy shadows cast by the rocks and by the stunted trees behind us. With the passing of the lion a new stillness had fallen upon the vicinity. I have often noted that before. I have heard the African night literally filled with sound—the sounds of animals, of night birds, of insects—and at the roar of a lion every sound will cease. The animals move silently, if they move at all. The birds cease their squawking. Even insects stop their endless streams of sound. How strange it is that even creatures that have no need to fear a lion thus recognize his power.

For some time, consequently, after the lion had passed, we saw nothing, but little by little the insect sounds recommenced. Back in the trees the night birds regained their confidence. Finally a jackal appeared, while others yapped in the distance, and presently a herd of zebra, twenty strong perhaps, came trooping toward the waterhole, their stripes brightly black and white in the moonlight.

Three or four drank at once, the others standing about, alert and ready to give the alarm. But no alarm was necessary, and presently they departed, passing three towering giraffe on the way.

The giraffe came up with fewer signs of fear than I would have expected them to show. Perhaps the herd of zebra had reassured them. At any rate, they wasted little time, and the smallest one drank first, the two taller animals standing with their heads a good fourteen feet above the ground, alert and on guard while their companion, his front feet stretched wide apart, thrust his little head down to the level of the water.

A giraffe's neck has always been one of the strangest things in Nature to me. And one of the strangest things about it is that it contains identically the same number of cervical vertebrae as an elephant's neck, or a dog's, or my own. And furthermore, despite all the neck with which Nature has presented this extraordinary animal, there was, apparently, no space available for any vocal cords. They are not there, at any rate, and the giraffe is, consequently, voiceless. But here we did hear one make a sound, and a good loud sound at that—he got water up his nose and throwing back his head he blew it out with a snort so loud it echoed up and down the donga.

The second giraffe did not stoop to drink until the first was ready to serve as sentry, but I must admit that from this point on, I did not see just what went on at the water-hole, for with the suddenness of an explosion we were startled by a most prodigious snort in our rear, and looking quickly about, we found that, contrary to all the rules of rhino etiquette, two of these ugly old beasts had come up behind us without a sound that we had heard, and now were at the other side of our little level place, not a bit more than thirty yards away. Furthermore, the start that first snort had given us had caused us to turn about very abruptly, with the result—because of the noise we made, no doubt—that they snorted again and charged.

We had no desire to shoot, but neither did we care to run the risk of being impaled on their horns. We were on our feet instantly, but it was Osa who gave the orders.

"Quick!" she cried. "This way!"

And off she dashed, with the rest of us after her, along the edge of the "step" at the top of which we had been sitting. We ran for twenty feet, perhaps, the rhinos, as yet, giving no sign that their charge was a fake.

"Jump!" cried Osa, setting the example.

It was not more than five or six feet down to the top of the "step" below us, and we jumped. But as we landed we were startled anew, for with a "yap" that almost froze our blood, a hyena scuttled away from us, and disappeared in a split second. How close we came to jumping on him none of us were able to determine. Probably it was not so close as it seemed then, but as for me, that yap seemed almost as if it came from right beside my knees.

It took us a minute or so to collect ourselves, and then, when we looked back, we found that having come up to within twenty feet or so of where we had been, the rhinos had turned about and trotted off.

But already the eastern sky was turning ever so faintly pale. In another hour the sun would rise, so we set off for camp. Anyway, we wanted breakfast and a few hours' sleep.

That first night at the waterhole had shown us, beyond

any doubt, that the country was filled with game, and the semi-vacation that we had planned turned out to be a period of fascinating work, during which we were more than usually successful with our cameras. As a matter of fact, the opportunities were so numerous and our facilities for taking advantage of them were so limited that we often separated, each with a task of his own to occupy him. On one occasion, when Osa was to spend the day alone in a blind at a waterhole while I was to do the same at another waterhole three miles or so away, she had an adventure about which I like to tease her yet.

I left her at her blind early in the morning, after having set up her camera, and having made arrangements to come back for her about sunset, I went off on my own task. The day passed more or less as usual, except that giraffe and kongoni, zebra and gazelle, seemed more than usually numerous. I managed to get quantities of pictures of them before the heat waves began to make photography impossible.

Photography in Africa is not satisfactory during the middle of the day. Heat waves become so heavy that pictures made at a distance of over fifty feet are wavy, giving an out-of-focus effect that is not pleasing. Then again, shadows under the eyes of animals do not give them expression, so, unless the subject is of more than ordinary interest or is something I cannot get again, I never attempt pictures during the hours when the sun is overhead. The few hours after the sun comes up, or three hours before it

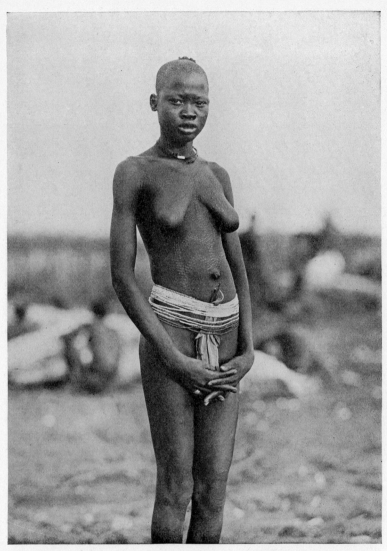

YOUNG LADY OF THE NILE. A native girl who lives along the upper Nile in Uganda. The abrasions on her body and face may be of three kinds. One is a tribal design, another is adornment, and a third is a primitive kind of vaccination. Many tribes cut the skin and rub in herbs as a preventative or cure of disease. It is probable that in this case the designs on the body are adornment, and on the cheeks tribal marks. The dress of leaves is fresh each morning.

A PAIR OF TOPI. A pair of topi watching a cheetah, while I crept up from the rear and photographed them with a long-focus lens. This attitude is typical of the topi and kongoni; they become so intent upon watching some object ahead that it is comparatively easy to come up on them from behind.

sets, are the best. During these hours the shadows are long and, beautiful backlight effects often are possible. So I read awhile, ate my lunch, and finally took a nap that lasted for two or three hours. Then again, as the sun slid down toward the horizon and the heat waves disappeared, I obtained more pictures as new herds trooped up to drink, and finally, quite satisfied with a quiet, though more than usually successful, day, I saw the two boys who were to come for me as they made their way across a little donga near by.

We gathered up my belongings, and tramped off toward camp, detouring in order to get Osa on the way.

My own day had been so quietly successful that I really gave no thought to the possibility of hers having been anything else. The result was that no one could have been more surprised than I to find Osa with her gun in her hands, and her mind obviously made up to do or die, though for what reason I could not for the moment imagine.

"What's the matter?" I demanded when I reached her.

"Watch out, Martin," she replied. "There's a lion right behind the blind. He's been around for hours, and I've been afraid to go out. It seemed to me a little while ago that he was actually trying to get on the blind."

A lion-like grunt from behind a near-by thorn bush punctuated her account.

"There!" she whispered. "Hear him?"

I straightened up and looked toward the thorn bush. The grunt had sounded like that of a lion, it is true, but it had a character of its own beside. I was not certain, but I thought I knew just what had made the sound, and as I stared, I saw, through an opening in the branches of the thorn bush, the characteristic jerk and the beady eye of a cock ostrich.

I laughed, and the two-legged "lion" departed at top speed.

"I'm surprised at you," I told Osa. "Don't you know an ostrich when you hear one?"

"Oh, Martin," she complained, as she crawled out of the narrow opening in the blind, "I *know* you'll tell everybody."

And the truth is that I have told it more than once, but then, so has she.

But if her experience with the ostrich had not been dangerous, she had one a few days later that was. We had come back to camp one evening more than usually hungry and Osa, who is not only the equal of any man in the field but is also the one who makes camp livable and meals a delight, turned to immediately get out the supplies for the cook. We had had a little grass hut built in which to store our chop boxes, and she went in, as she always did, intent on getting whatever it was she was after.

I do not know how long she was gone, for I was busy with my lenses, but presently she was standing beside me with the whitest face I ever saw.

"Martin," she began. "Martin—"

170

That something was wrong I saw in a moment, and I dropped a lens into its case with a thump.

"What's the matter?" I demanded.

"Whew!" she began, and shook her head. "I just had a narrow escape."

"From what?" I asked.

"Well," she went on, "I went to get something from the chop boxes, and just as I put my hand on the lid, I saw a big black something right behind it. I was paralyzed."

"What was it?" I demanded.

"A cobra," she announced, "and he raised his head three or four feet into the air and spread his hood, and looked at me. I was afraid to move for fear he'd strike, so I *didn't* move, and presently he lowered his head and went out the door. And he was ten feet long if he was an inch."

She sat down in a chair in order to collect herself, while I called the boys and told them to find the creature, but though they took their big knives, and hunted for an hour, there was no sign of him. He had slipped away through the grass and the thorn bush.

As I have explained, the natives who roam this region are mostly the Lumbwa, and we saw them often. They came into camp on any pretext or with no pretext at all, and were a fine upstanding lot, despite their smell. But the numerous wild animals that delighted us were a nuisance to them, for they had their herds and themselves to protect, and the rhinos and lions made that difficult. As a matter of fact, however, the lions were not bothering them, for there were too many zebras and antelopes about to make it necessary for a lion to kill the natives' cattle. The rhinos, however, were another story, and we were told that only a few days before we arrived two old women had been killed by these wrinkled old fellows. Furthermore, every now and then the rhinos came too close to the natives' manyettas for comfort, and before we had been in camp for a week the Lumbwas decided to declare war on the rhinos and run them out of the country.

The natives of Kenya Colony are not permitted to have firearms, but these Lumbwa, I am free to admit, do not greatly need them. They are marvelous spearsmen, and do not hesitate to attack lions or rhinos, despite the fact that for arms they have nothing but their beautiful, six-foot spears, and their long, sword-like knives.

The East African spear is a beautiful, symmetrical weapon, but it is made of very soft metal, easily bent, and difficult to keep sharp. When a native thinks he will need his spear, however, he will spend hours in sharpening it, despite the fact that it will not stay sharp long. Furthermore, it will bend so easily that it requires a great deal of skill in throwing to make it effective. A person who does not understand its use is apt to use too much force in throwing, with the result that it does not go straight and is bent all out of shape, often without penetrating far enough to do any harm. A native who is proficient in its use, however, balances it with three fingers and "follows through" with his body, with the result that it flies out on a perfect line,

and enters the body of the animal with extraordinary penetrating power. I once saw a native pierce a lion entirely
through the body with a foot of spear protruding on the
opposite side from where it entered. It is with these spears,
and with big, buffalo-hide shields that they often take to
the fields after lion and rhino. Furthermore, this is no mimic
warfare. They mean business, and are successful in a large
percentage of their encounters.

It is no mean feat for a group of naked hunters to attack
a lion and kill it with their spears. But it is a still greater
feat for a man to accomplish such a task alone, and many
a Lumbwa warrior has done just that. Lion-skin head-
dresses are not uncommon among them. One sees them
being worn in every manyetta, yet that is a sign the wearer,
singlehanded, has slain his lion with his spear—no light
honor, it seems to me.

But as I have said, the lions were not making trouble—
it was the rhinos, and when we heard that the natives were
going rhino-spearing we decided that the chance to make
some highly unusual pictures was far too good to miss. Consequently we went with them.

The surface waterholes were mostly dried up, and every
day the animals were forced to dig deeper to quench their
thirst. Now a rhino is not built for digging. On account of
his short legs, about as much sand runs back in the hole as
he digs out, so in this district they were mostly using the
same waterholes that the Lumbwa were, because the natives
were naturally using the water that was easiest to get.

It is a peculiar thing, however, that only three miles away there was the Guasa Nyiro River with good, clear water. Yet both the natives and the animals preferred the slightly alkali water in the muddy waterholes. I have noticed this time after time in my wanderings over Africa. Animals will always go to a nasty, muddy outcropping of water rather than to clear streams near by. Perhaps it is the salty taste of poor water that they like best.

In this case, however, we joined the natives at their man-yetta, though we failed to reach it until the preparatory ceremonies were about over. Natives never seem able to do anything of importance without a ceremony of some kind, usually dancing and singing. But though we were too late for that, we were in time to follow the band of warriors as they took the field, their great oval shields painted brightly in meaningless designs, their handsome spears, each with a blade three feet in length, carried upright in their hands, and their knives slung, sword-like, at their waists.

So close had the rhinos come to the village that we had gone only a mile or two before the first was sighted across the grass of a bit of open country. It was, of course, our desire to get our camera set up in an advantageous place before the attack began, but the rhino had no particular desire to accommodate us, and though the Lumbwa was quite willing to do so, the excitement of the hunt and their desire to come to grips drove all thought of us from their minds.

They started out conservatively enough, and spread out

174

in a line as they advanced toward the rhino. The old fellow was all of a quarter of a mile away when we first spied him, and until the Lumbwa had come up to within a hundred yards or so he failed, apparently, to realize his danger. But then, quite suddenly, he seemed to catch their scent, despite the fact that they were advancing upwind. Some eddy in the breeze, perhaps, carried it to him, though, goodness knows, a Lumbwa can be scented, even by a white man, at some distance, and a score or more of them are hardly to be missed by even the poorest nose.

Now up to this point all our arrangements to take pictures had gone perfectly, though the distance was still too great and the thorn bushes were too numerous to make photography possible. But no sooner had the rhino let out his first prodigious snort than the Lumbwa, very naturally, forgot all the requests that I had made for coöperation, and were intent only on getting that rhino, quite regardless of what our camera might do. Then again, they were anxious to show off their bravery before the white people.

Up went the rhino's tail, for without that preliminary move a rhino seems unable to do anything. Another snort! A doubtful half charge for a few steps. Another snort!

The Lumbwa were going forward now, no longer trying to keep from alarming the beast. They did not run, but they went forward unhesitatingly. The rhino trotted angrily in a circle and stopped. He came forward for a dozen steps and stopped. He backed up for a step or two, and snorted again.

All this time the Lumbwa were advancing, and now they

were within fifty yards. The rhino stamped and snorted until I saw the dust fly up from the dry ground. He raised his head and lowered it, trotted a little to one side—stopped —snorted again, and in another moment had lowered his head and charged.

I turned the switch on the camera, knowing perfectly well that I would get nothing of value. I was too far off and the grass and bushes hid most of what took place. But suddenly the Lumbwa were leaping through the grass as the rhino came toward them. It seemed for a moment as if one native was about to be impaled on the beast's long horn, but in another instant the fellow had leaped aside and had thrown his spear powerfully into the rhino's side. I saw it land there while the animal charged on through the shifting, dancing, spear-throwing group of natives. A spear glanced harmlessly across the beast's back. Another struck him full on his horn and fell to the ground. The first spear, bent into a great semi-circle, as I learned later, fell from his side, and another, thrown from a distance of twenty feet, landed, quivering, in his shoulder.

All this takes time to tell, but it took little enough time to happen, and now, conscious, no doubt, that he had met his masters, the rhino whirled about, almost striking a native as he did so, and ran as I have never seen a rhino run before, until he disappeared from sight among the thorn bush half a mile away. The natives pursued him with all the determination in the world until they, too, disappeared from sight, leaving us with our cameras, with which we could

THE HIGHEST MOUNTAIN IN AFRICA. Mt. Kilimanjaro during one of the rare times when the peak is visible. It is 19,450 feet above sea level and the highest mountain in Africa.

BESIDE THE PYGMY FOREST. Our landing strip at the edge of the Ituri Forest in the Belgian Congo. Within a few miles, in the dense forest, is the home of thousands of the pygmy people, who dislike coming out into the hot sunlight. When moving about they follow the contour of the forest rather than walk across a clearing.

make no such speed, while we complained of our bad luck in seeing such a sight and failing, so almost completely, to get it on our film.

Three rhinos were attacked this morning, but we saw less of the second two engagements than we had seen of the first. As a matter of fact they all got away, or so the natives told us. Still, it had been a sight worth seeing, and one that would not fail to impress the bravery of the Lumbwa on one's mind.

That night I talked to the Lumbwa and told them that they would not get the baksheesh I promised them unless I got pictures, and Osa suggested that she go with them with her rifle, not to shoot, but to protect them in case a dangerous situation arose, for by doing so they could do their work much closer to the cameras.

The Lumbwa knew they would have small hope of killing the rhino, and they had no particular desire to do so. Their only object was to push the beasts back, away from their waterholes.

Now the Lumbwa is not modest. He loudly tells everyone how brave he is and on the following days we had a chance to look into the matter. Of course, our past experience with them had taught us that they really are brave, but never before had we seen them attack rhino.

On the following morning we were in the thorn bush again at daybreak, Osa, Fritz and I leading, my camera bearers and the Lumbwa following. Within a short distance we came upon two rhino, an enormous old cow and her

177

half-grown son. Wind and sun were right, so I set up the cameras. The Lumbwa were anxious to go, but, as the rhino were slowly grazing our way, I cautioned the Lumbwa to wait until I gave the signal. Then, when the two animals were only seventy or eighty feet away, I gave the word, and forward rushed the spearsmen. The rhino, taken by surprise, raised their heads and snorted. Their little beady eyes seemed to flash in anger, and they held their ground as the Lumbwa advanced. This discouraged the natives. By all the rules of the game the two rhino should have acted quite differently. They should either have charged or run, thus giving the spearsmen the cue as to what to do. But two rhinos snorting and seemingly defying them was something new, so the Lumbwa stopped, undecided on just how to handle the situation. Then, however, the rhino made the decision. They both charged, and charged fast. The Lumbwa threw their spears in a panic. None touched either rhino, and every brave native came running back to us. Osa stood her ground with her rifle. Fritz dropped the still camera he was using and grabbed his rifle. But the rhino suddenly changed their minds. They whirled and dashed off to one side, passing within fifteen feet of us. And now, the Lumbwa were after them. Hindered by the thorn bush, however, they were too slow and the rhino easily made their escape. But we had secured some good pictures this time, and Osa had again demonstrated her theory that a rhino will usually lose his nerve when he gets close enough to distinguish his object. We had discovered, too, that the

Lumbwa were brave up to a certain point, but that they were also sensible. When they saw nearly four tons of rhino charging down on them with their sharp horns ready for business, they, quite properly, decided that the protection of our guns was better than the protection of their spears and shields.

For several days we followed the rhino with the Lumbwa. Every day we saw from ten to twenty, though generally the rhino saw or heard us or got our scent before we were close enough for pictures. Sometimes we did get good pictures and we learned a lot about the bravery of the Lumbwa. We found that when a rhino charged the natives were immediately upon him and ready to battle. But if a rhino stopped and snorted and defied them, they stopped. A rhino standing still, watching on all sides and ready for battle was a different thing from a rhino coming from a distance. In the latter case the natives could attack from the sides, but they did not know what to do about a defiant rhino.

One day about noon we found a young cow asleep under a tree, and before I could stop them the Lumbwa all rushed in with the idea of killing it before it woke up. That did not suit Osa, however. She did not consider it sporting, so she rushed up behind them and just as the first spear was thrown, she fired in the air, frightening both the Lumbwa and the rhino. The Lumbwa could not make out what had happened, and during their uncertainty the rhino was off as fast as her short legs could carry her.

But the same afternoon the natives did manage to spear

179

one of the big brutes. We had the cameras set up, the Lumbwa were standing with their spears ready, and a fine big bull was slowly grazing towards us. We were so still that I could hear my watch ticking, and this time I had instructed the spearsmen to wait with me until I gave the word. On and on the rhino came. He was within thirty feet when I gave the word, and then out rushed the Lumbwa, throwing most of their spears wild, but one hit its mark squarely. The spear remained in the animal as he whirled and ran. We followed, for we try to make it our policy not to let a wounded animal get away. The rhino was almost instantly out of sight in the thorn bush, but he was easy to follow by the blood spoor. For three miles we followed through that boiling sun, then came out on the edge of a small dry swamp covered with waist-high dead grass and reeds. There was the rhino, but he was moving slowly, weak from the loss of blood. We followed and were soon close enough so that he could hear us. He stopped and Osa moved forward with her rifle. I just barely had time to get my camera ready when the rhino started toward Osa in little goose steps. He stopped and snorted, whirled and turned around. Then he started slowly towards Osa again, gaining speed as he got closer. He was almost on top of her when she fired, and he dropped. And right there Osa did a foolish thing. Without waiting to see what would happen next she turned to me and shouted, "I got him." I was horrified, for though the beast had fallen, it was plain to me that he was not dead, and there was Osa, with her back toward the

A **TROPHY LION**. A fine lion and several lionesses. They were asleep in the shade of the tree when we came upon them. The lionesses paid us little attention, but the big lion was nervous, as though he knew that he would make a fine trophy for a sportsman.

LARGE HERD OF GIRAFFE. There is no doubt that there are more giraffe on the Serengetti Plains than any other place in Africa. We once counted 130 in a herd. Their colors vary from a faded yellow to very dark sable. Lions kill many, although a giraffe can put up a stiff fight with his powerful forelegs.

old fellow as he struggled to his feet, while I, at the camera, had no gun.

"Look out!" I shouted, and she turned about, her rifle ready again. But the rhino had been hard hit. He did not charge. Instead, he turned, ran a few steps, and toppled over—dead.

8

ABOUT five miles from our camp a colony of baboons lived, on the banks of the Guaso Nyiro River. At this point the river is not large and during the dry season there are many rocks that stand above the water and make a sort of series of irregular stepping stones by which the baboons and the monkeys can cross back and forth at will. On one side of the stream, too, there is a rocky cliff, the face of which is broken by ledges and even little holes resembling caves. It was on these ledges and in these holes that the baboons stayed at night.

Now baboons, as I learned long ago, are forever being menaced by leopards, which prowl around at night when the baboons are asleep. I am of the opinion that baboons form a large part of the leopard's diet, for the baboon is usually a tree dweller and the leopard is a very fine climber of trees.

But here on the rocky ledges and in the holes no leopard could get at the baboons, with the result that this had probably been the home of baboons for generations. At any rate it was an excellent place in which to photograph them, for they would not leave the vicinity of their homes unless they were very badly molested. Accordingly I had a small tent brought from camp, together with some provisions, a couple of extra beds, a couple of spare tripods and enough light camp equipment so that Osa and I could come here when we had the time and spend the night. Two boys were left in charge, and it proved that this was a wise move, for the baboons gradually got used to the tent and us, and every day were less disturbed by our appearance. I also built several rough blinds at different points, and even had one in a tree-top.

From that time on Osa and I often visited this camp in order to spend a day in the blinds. Sometimes, too, we spent the night in order to be on hand for the good morning light, and I can safely say that the experiences we had with these baboons were among the most interesting and were certainly the funniest that we have ever had with wild animals. Every move they made was either interesting or comic, and there must have been two thousand of them.

Osa and I have always insisted that the baboon is the most intelligent of the monkey family, though that is a dangerous thing to say, for many people confuse the monkeys with the apes and so mistake our meaning. But here we had a chance to get better acquainted and see if we were right. At first they were all just baboons, but gradually we were able to distinguish some of them by their individualities, and we even went so far as to name a few. For instance, one fine big fellow seemed to be sort of a head man. He had his own particular tree crotch in which he would sit for hours at a time, and he was the easiest of all to photograph, for we could get closer to him, and sometimes we even photographed him without going into the blinds. He was so big and fat and lazy that he hated to move, and he was terribly self-conscious if we stared at him for any length of time. He would stare back as long as he could and then, to cover his self-consciousness, he would yawn. Sometimes he would yawn so much that he would get us to yawning, and when we laughed at him it would make him so angry that he would bristle up his hair and swear at us. I'll swear that he could swear, too, and his voice was placed on different sound levels that gave the impression that he was using every swear word ever invented.

We were soon able to distinguish different families, as well as different individuals, for we would see the same groups together day after day. The mothers and fathers would often cuff the youngsters until the little fellows would roll over and over, screaming to the limit of their lungs. To such family affairs as these were, none of the others would pay any attention, but sometimes a member of one family would cuff a youngster of another family, and then there was a battle. These inter-family fights were often quite exciting and the noise was terrible. One would think they were tearing each other to pieces, until suddenly the fight would stop as quickly as it started, each family going about its business as though nothing had happened.

We found the fathers were very good to their youngsters, holding them as much as the mothers, allowing the babies to wool them and fall over them without seeming to care.

MIGRATING HERD OF ELEPHANTS. Part of a herd of hundreds that we flew over near Mombasa on the East Coast of Kenya. This is not their regular stamping ground. They were on migration, and very hard to photograph on account of the dense bushes and trees. It was only by flying very low that we got any pictures at all, and then our flight was so swift that most of the pictures showed movement.

A STUDY IN CONTRAST. Orangi, our head-man, and two little pygmy girls. Orangi is five feet seven in height, while the girls are of average pygmy size. From measurements we made, we decided the average pygmy height to be about three feet eleven inches.

The mothers, on the other hand, always seemed to be worried about the children. If a baby strayed too far away, the mother would run and grab it and pull it back, not too gently sometimes, and the baby would let out a howl as though it were being killed. Baby baboons are awful crybabies.

As I have said, we soon had names for the more distinguished baboons. The old fellow who yawned we called John. A small, ugly baby we called Mickey Mouse. A young male with a scar across his cheek we named Scar Face Al. An old lady we called Grandmother, and so on.

The distance between the river and the cliff was about a hundred feet, but between the two there were bushes and trees among which the baboons spent most of every day. They always seemed to find something to eat in those trees, too. What it was I don't know, for it seemed that they should have eaten every edible thing in a few days, but somehow they always found something, and they were remarkably fat, sleek, and healthy. In fact, they were the finest baboons we have ever seen. It is possible, of course, that at times they went further away for food, but with their enormous curiosity they seemed to be unable to tear themselves from the place while we were around.

As time went on they became more and more accustomed to us. After a time we could even go to the water's edge on our side of the stream, in clear sight of the colony, and they would come to the water's edge at the other side and watch us. If I was working with my cameras they were very much interested, but if I stopped and looked at them, most of them became nervous and ran back to the trees, where most of their activities were centered, though the whole place seemed like a veritable baboon city to us—so much so, in fact, that we called it "Baboona." The way life flowed back and forth along the river's edge often reminded us of a civilized city. Each baboon passing and repassing seemed to have some really definite place he was bound for, and some real business that was demanding his attention. As a matter of fact, they came and went for absolutely no reason at all.

Now Osa is somewhat of a tom-boy. She has all the imagination of a mischievous kid, so I was not surprised when one day she appeared on the scene with a sling shot such as all boys use. She had made it out of two elastic garters—a crude affair, but it worked.

"Now," she remarked, "watch old John," and, with a pebble in the sling shot, she took careful aim. Her aim was good, too, for she hit him squarely in the side. John jumped about three feet and let out a tremendous yell. He scratched himself vigorously, parting the hair as if to see the extent of his injury. Then he looked belligerently around, scowling ferociously and baring his teeth until his long fangs gleamed in the sunlight. Had any other baboon even looked at him I am sure there would have been a fight, but no one paid any attention to him, so he was forced to fall back on his baboon profanity.

Elated with her success, and laughing until tears ran

down her cheeks, Osa decided to try again. Waiting until John was looking away, she fired another pebble, but it went wild. The next one stung him on the ear, and this time he was furious. He jumped from the tree fork, his hair bristling as he stalked stiff-legged up and down the well-worn path along the river's edge. He shook his head, sitting down several times to scratch it with his hind leg, all the time swearing and barking at the top of his voice. The others seemed to realize that he was in a dangerous mood, too, for they fled, leaving the path to John. It was fully thirty minutes before he settled down, but for an hour he scratched his head and muttered to himself.

One day we saw a mother teaching her baby to climb trees. The wrinkled little fellow had probably been born only a few days before, but he was able to hold on so tightly with his clenched little hands and feet that the mother already seemed to be getting tired of having her hair pulled. She would stand it as long as she could and then would try to shift him to a new position. This would frighten the baby and he would hold on to his mother's hair more tightly than ever, whereupon she would cuff him so soundly that he would be forced to let go. Then she would grab him and place him in the fork of a tree where he had to hold on. Having done that she would climb above him and he would have to climb in order to reach her. This happened again and again, the baby squealing all the time, but finally he stopped crying and seemed to get the idea. He never seemed to learn not to pull his mother's hair, however. Each time she would pull him off she would scratch herself where he had been holding on.

Baboons only a few months old were always playing, wooling one another, and having sham fights. The others would pay no attention to this until one would start screaming when he was treated a little too roughly by the other youngsters. Then for a few minutes there would be a bedlam of yelling as the older baboons rushed in, thinking, no doubt, that their children were being harmed. These fights would go on all day, and from the sounds one would imagine that the beasts would injure one another, but I never saw a sign of blood or wounds, with the exception of two older ones that had healed scars on their faces.

One afternoon Osa and I were particularly entertained by a mother and her baby. The mother was squatting on the ground pulling the bark from a small broken limb. The baby was playing about, but seemed inclined to stray too far. Every minute or so, consequently, the mother would grab it and pull it back to her side. After a good bit of this the baby became peevish and finally, when she grabbed it again, lifted its little fist and struck her on the nose. It was probably an involuntary movement. Perhaps it had no idea of striking the mother and had just happened to throw up its little fist in time to connect with her nose. Nevertheless, she must have thought it was done deliberately and with malice aforethought, for she grabbed the youngster by the tail, held it up and boxed its ears until it screamed. Father then came walking up and stood within a few feet, watching the operation, grunting and acting as though he were talking to the mother in a low voice. He may have been agreeing with mother that baby needed chastising for being so fresh, but one could easily imagine him saying something of this sort: "Now, mother, don't lose your temper. He is only a little chap, after all." But presently she was finished with him, and the poor little baby walked off a few feet and sat there sobbing as though its heart were broken.

Osa and I would sometimes be away from the baboons for several days while we were photographing rhino. Then, when we thought we had stirred the rhino up too much and had them on the alert, we would leave them for a few days and return to the baboons. The two boys who were supposed to guard the small tent while we were away sometimes got tired of sitting around and often wandered up or down the river. Several times the baboons got into the tent during their absence and nearly wrecked everything inside. This gave us an idea which we proceeded to carry out. We built a blind about three hundred feet from the tent, set up two cameras with long focus 17- and 24-inch lenses focused on the tent, slept in the blind that night, and all next day photographed the coming and going of the baboons around the tent. We left food stuffs inside some of the chop boxes, placed other food inside and around the tent, and placed a large mirror and a small hand mirror where they could see them. That was a day of great interest. Old John seemed to have the most curiosity. Without the least hesitation he went across the rocks in the stream, went all around the tent and very quickly found the food which he proceeded to eat. Then a mother came along with her baby, and the little fellow was more curious than almost any other. He was especially curious about the chop boxes, but mother was worried that he would get into a trap, I suppose, for she pulled him out every time he got into a box. Usually she was gentle with him, but when he kept insisting on getting into a certain box she cuffed his ears.

John was very much interested in the big square mirror, and I would have made some interesting pictures of his reactions had it not been for the fact that he knocked it over. It fell face down and he lost interest, but he did become interested in the small round hand mirror we had left. We laughed until we cried as we watched him reach behind it trying to find the other good-looking baboon. He showed no signs of anger—only curiosity, but we never did get that mirror back, for he took it with him across the stream and I suppose he is still looking at it and trying to find that other baboon.

On our side of the river were quite a good many ground monkeys. They never crossed to the baboon side of the stream, perhaps because they were afraid, although being wonderful jumpers they could easily have gone over from rock to rock had they wanted to. Strange to say, these little monkeys were not a bit interested in our tent and never molested anything.

One day Osa and I were nearly asleep during the middle of the day, when we became aware of an unusual amount of screaming among the baboons. We looked up from our blind to see two spotted hyenas preparing to cross the stream. They were in such a hurry that I felt certain that something had frightened them, and, of course, they frightened the baboons, which, for the most part, ran into the trees, although some of the older ones held their ground with their hair all bristled up. The hyenas swam and waded across the stream and then ran squarely through the baboon settlement and disappeared.

Now I have no great fondness for hyenas, but I was especially angry at these two. For some time I had been trying to get a really good action picture of the baboons, and on the very day that these hyenas appeared I had my arrangements complete. I was merely waiting until the light was right later in the afternoon before trying it out. I had worked really hard and had finally managed to place several motion picture cameras in the trees and on different points on the ground, all with lenses of different focal lengths, and all focused on the rocks over which the baboons crossed every day. My idea was to get a bunch on our side of the river, frighten them, and then pull the strings that ran from the blind to the cameras, thus releasing triggers and starting the cameras. Two of the cameras were to make slow motion, too, and altogether I hoped to get an interesting and exciting set of movies from different angles as the baboons rushed back across the river.

It was this plan that I was afraid the hyenas had upset, but as events now developed I got what I wanted, but in a different and highly unexpected way. I was still grumbling to Osa about the hyenas when a much greater commotion began among the baboons, and in another moment two fine leopards appeared—a big male, and a smaller female. The female made several leaps at the baboons, while the big male walked up and down almost like a caged animal. Then the female dashed into the bushes and out came the two hyenas like a streak of lightning, and away they went down the river, mooing and whimpering as they ran. We lost track of the female leopard—she may have followed the hyenas, but I don't know. The big male remained in plain sight, however, stalking up and down, snarling, and making short rushes after the baboons now and then. The whole colony was now in a turmoil, of course. Mothers were holding their babies tight and getting to the highest branches. Others ran for the protection of the cliff and probably hid in the little caves. Old John was right in the midst of things and was the most courageous one of all. Then, when the leopard took a leap back into the bushes, out came scores and scores of baboons, and, with John leading, they started a mad rush across the river. They were in a panic by now, and they came in such a rush that they jumped on top of one another. Some fell in the water and swam. Mothers, hindered by the weight of their babies, tried to leap to the rocks, but fell short and were forced to swim. One mother saw that she could not reach the rock and tried to turn around in the air, naturally getting a good ducking. Luckily for us, a great many of them crossed

THE HAPPIEST SAVAGES ON EARTH. Vern, myself, and Osa with a typical group of pygmies. The happiest little savages on earth, the pygmies never think of tomorrow or yesterday, all that matters to them is today. I never saw them quarrel or fight among themselves.

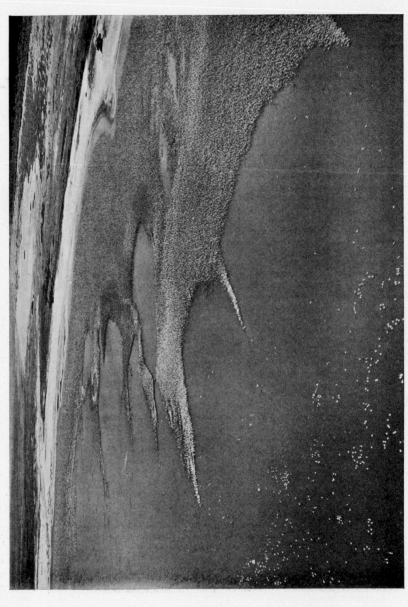

FLAMINGOES BY THE BILLION ON LAKE NAIVASHA. Since it is approximately thirty miles around the shore line of this lake, and since all along the shore the birds are living as shown in the picture, one can get a good idea of their enormous numbers. Seen from the air, they make a beautiful pink border in a setting of blue or green, according to the time of day.

at the rocks where we had the cameras trained, although scores of others swam up and down the river, and some probably remained in their caves along the cliff.

Evidently a baboon's memory is very short, however, for when they had crossed the stream all alarm seemed to leave them. The leopard did not follow them, it is true, but they had started out as if they were utterly panic-stricken. Instead of going on and on, however, they remained in the country of the monkeys, and these little creatures naturally resented the intrusion. The result was that a new war started promptly. Led by a brave little monkey mother with her baby hanging to her, the indignant monkeys tried to force the invaders out of their country, but the newcomers did not take the little monkeys very seriously, though they did worry John. As I have explained, he was big. I believe, as a matter of fact, that he was by far the largest baboon I have ever seen. A full-grown baboon will, perhaps, not usually weigh over seventy pounds, but both Osa and I are agreed that John would weigh at least a hundred. Probably we were fooled by his long glossy hair, but anyway a hundred is our story and we are going to stick to it. Well, John was so big and so powerful, and his fangs were so long that there is no doubt in my mind that he could have torn a man to pieces if he had come to grips with one, and he certainly could have killed those little monkeys without an effort if he had wanted to. But repulsing the attacks of the monkeys was a game with John. He was enjoying himself. The trouble was that the little monkeys were in deadly earnest. John made rush after rush at the little mother that led the attack, but she held her ground with the most surprising spirit. And finally John was forced to carry out his bluff or back away. He chose to back away, and all the monkeys took after him. He went up trees and they followed. He picked them off branches and threw them down like bananas, yet they followed to the top of a tree and some of them got so tangled together that they all lost their balance and came tumbling down together.

This went on for over an hour, the little monkeys seemingly as fresh as ever. But John was getting winded, and he was getting little or no help, for the other baboons were busy picking up the bits of food that we had scattered around that morning. Thus the "battle" had degenerated into an attack by the monkeys on John alone. There was a grass hut near by that had been used by our two boys, and to the top of this went John, with the monkeys still after him. By this time all the food had been picked up and the baboons were scattering. Furthermore, John was probably disgusted with the monkeys, for he leaped from the hut and began a second flight, followed by the baboons that had not already disappeared. They crossed a slight hill and then we lost sight of them, while the little ground monkeys chattered and hurried about as though they thought they had won an important battle.

Osa and I had enjoyed all this immensely, and had exposed thousands of feet of film, but we felt sure that the baboons had been badly upset. We even thought that they might leave the country. We returned to our main camp, consequently, and did not come back again until the second day after the battle. What was our surprise then, however, to find that there was the city of Baboona carrying on as usual. Even John was in his usual perch in the crotch of his own tree and apparently all was well.

By this time we had used the same background so much that we decided to move down the river a quarter of a mile. We built a blind at a place where there were no trees or bushes in front of us, though we were flanked on both sides by heavy jungle. Our idea, now, was to bait the open space and perhaps get baboons concentrated before our cameras in greater numbers. As a further way of discouraging them from spreading out too much we sent our boys to block up the side trails with thorn bush. We planned to bait the open space and then make a single line of food along the trail all the way from the baboon city. This, if our plan worked, might lead almost the whole baboon colony to within range of our lenses.

That night we had several petrol tins of posho boiled into a thick mush, and the next morning we set out the bait as we had planned. It was not long before some of the baboons found the line of food on the trail, and when a baboon finds food he must talk about it. That immediately told the others about the food and quantities of them came trooping down to the clearing where several bushels of food were dumped in one spot. The fun began at once, of course. They naturally all wanted to eat, and the older baboons rushed in until they were heaped on top of one another. Yelling, screaming, and pulling, they scrambled for the food, while the youngsters got theirs by staying on the outside of the scrimmage and picking up the bits the others scattered. In fact I think they got the most food in the long run.

There must have been a hundred big baboons in that scramble for food, and certainly their antics were ridiculously amusing. I find it impossible to describe that seething, squalling, screaming tangle of baboons, but to see those old fellows pulling each other off by the legs and hair, only to be pulled off in their turn, was most ridiculous. And we were making marvelous pictures with lots of action. Several fights started and some tried to run away with others after them, to be stopped by our thorn bush walls. Then tangled groups of them went down and rolled over and over, while Osa and I were almost ready to do the same with laughter. But the food was disappearing, and presently it was gone, though for a time they continued to mill around to make sure no small bits were left. We examined them closely, now that the fight was over, and tried to count up the casualties. But look though we might there was not a sign of blood or wounds, despite the fact that when the scramble was on the noise and fighting had made us think that some of them would surely be seriously injured. Once they were convinced that the food was really gone, they trooped off upstream again, headed for home.

"Those will be marvelous pictures, Martin," Osa remarked, as I began to pack up my equipment.

WILDEBEEST. Wildebeest on the Serengetti Plains in Tanganyika. This picture was made just as the animals put on an extra burst of speed when we were close to the ground. After we had passed over them, I saw that they had stopped and were looking around as though wondering what had frightened them.

GREAT HERD OF ZEBRA. During the migration periods in Tanganyika, the plains are crowded with millions of game. The different species herd together mostly, as in this scene of zebra. During this time lions, hyenas, and jackals go in and out of the herds with the game paying little attention to them. Apparently, the game know when the carnivorous animals seek to kill

Over African Jungles

I opened the door of my camera, certain that she was right, but the next moment I was a highly disappointed man, for one glance told me that the film had broken when the camera had started. I had not exposed a single foot of film, and had failed to get what was, I am certain, the funniest animal picture a camera ever had an opportunity to record.

We were busy almost every hour that we spent in the thorn bush country, and every day we saw and photographed animals by the score. Sometimes we photographed them by hundreds, and one day, when the heat waves were rocking the trees and hills and animals about until, with a little imagination, one could almost have got seasick over it, I saw a herd of giraffe that made me wonder if I had gone quite mad. Four or five hundred yards from where I was sitting in the shade of a tent fly lay an expanse of sand upon which the sun, no doubt, beat down with exceptional power, for from it the heat waves were wavering up with more than their usual energy. Just beyond this sandy place lay a scattering of low trees, between which the grass grew thick.

I was half dozing in the heat, and doing nothing in particular, when suddenly I noticed seven giraffe just beyond that patch of sand. But such giraffe as those I had never seen before. A giraffe fourteen or fifteen feet tall is no miracle. One of sixteen or even seventeen feet would, I suppose, be no impossibility even in these days. But those giraffe, if I am any judge of height, stood all of fifty feet

197

tall, and stood quite plainly out there in the sunlight. I was so astounded for a moment that I could not believe my eyes, which was just as well, for suddenly they turned and moved away, and in another moment, having passed beyond the heat rays that rose from that overheated patch of sand, they shrank until they were quite ordinary as to size. I had to laugh, of course, for giraffe so tall as those had seemed to be are too ridiculous even to think about, much less to see, despite the fact that I had seen them.

I sat in my chair for an hour, hoping to see some other exaggerated freak of nature, but nothing came. I wonder what a rhino would have looked like if he had been magnified in the same extraordinary way.

Now Africa is a land where such mirages are not uncommon, but mirages are freaks of nature about which many ridiculous stories have been told. I have heard of travelers on tropical deserts seeing cities in the mirage. I have heard of their seeing camel caravans, lakes, rivers, and pools with natives drinking, all in the same way, but I don't believe a word of these miracles. I have been on many of the world's deserts and I have seen many mirages, but a mirage is part heat wave and part imagination. It is built up entirely by heated air. On the horizon the mirage does give the effect of water, and any tree or bush or animal between the horizon and the person viewing it is distorted. Mostly it enlarges such objects, but sometimes it diminishes them. Sometimes an animal is distorted all out of shape so that it can resemble anything your imagination causes it to. One definite thing is that things beyond the horizon are not seen in the mirage, so that the story of a mirage picking up things long distances away and bringing them to you is, in my opinion, all bosh. It is safe to say that a mirage in which water seems to appear cannot be at a greater distance than six or seven miles, and nothing is ever seen in a mirage except things that are actually between the horizon and the observer. But even without mirages we saw a great deal that was interesting.

Hyenas were, of course, forever to be seen and heard. Leopards were more than numerous enough, too, and lions were about. We did not see a great many, it is true, but we heard them every night. All of them, though, kept well clear of camp except the hyenas, which always had to be guarded against when we were away. Everything with leather on it has to be kept most carefully guarded against these creatures. They seem to take especial delight in chewing the leather from binoculars or camera cases, or anything of the kind, and a leather belt seems almost to be a special tidbit to a hyena that can get one. Consequently, whenever we left camp unguarded, we were careful to lock all such things up, for we have had many leather belongings ruined by hyenas in the past.

Two or three days still remained before we were to break camp when, after a more than usually hard day's work, we went to bed early. We were all tired, and though I remember being awakened by a lion roaring rather close to camp,

I thought little of it, and went to sleep again with no idea of danger.

Our camp was small, and, aside from the tent that Osa and I shared, the one that Fritz used, and the dining tent, consisted of only two or three grass huts, a camera tent, and several shelters, without sides, beneath which the boys slept, each with nothing more in the way of bedding than a tanned skin upon which to lie.

The lion's roar, as I have said, had disturbed me, but I had gone to sleep again without giving it a second thought, and slept, I suppose, for another hour or two, when suddenly a shriek from one of the boys awoke me with such a start that I found myself sitting upright before I realized I was awake.

Osa, too, was sitting up in her cot across the tent, for I could see her head silhouetted against the faint gray of the sloping canvas.

And no sooner had that boy's shriek awakened us than we heard the hurrying feet of some animal as it darted across our tent ropes, dragging something with it as it ran.

My blood ran cold. How could I have failed to take heed of that lion's roar? He could hardly have been more than a few hundred yards from camp, even then. And now— what?

Every one of the boys, by now, was yelling as if mad, and I distinctly heard them as they took out after the retreating animal and its prey. What had happened we could, of course, have no idea, but seizing our guns, and dashing

WARTHOG FIGHTING LEOPARD. Movie enlargement. The warthog attacked the leopard time after time and never once did the cat go for the pig. It is possible there is something obnoxious about a pig that is repulsive to a leopard; or the leopard may know by instinct that the pig's hide is so tough and strong, and his vital organs so well protected, that he would be a difficult animal to kill. The cats probably prefer the antelope because there is no fight—just easy killing.

TEN-PLACE PLANE; THIRTY-SIX PYGMIES. Pygmies lined up, hoping for a ride in the plane. They were not one bit interested in how the plane flew, but they did love to fly. We had to disappoint most of them because we did not have a large supply of gasoline. Once we had thirty-six of them packed inside.

from the tent in our pajamas, we heard the natives as they ran yelling after the beast and whatever it was he had seized.

Fritz was outside his tent, as well, with his rifle in his hands, wondering, as we were, what tragic thing had taken place. Every boy in camp had gone, and one of their shelters was knocked out of shape, telling us something we could not interpret. If that lion had slipped into camp and had taken one of the boys I never would forgive myself.

"Was it a lion, Fritz?" I asked.

"I don't know," he replied. "I didn't hear a thing until the boys yelled."

"Did he get one of the boys?" asked Osa in a hushed sort of voice. "Oh, Martin. We should have been more careful."

Off in the distance the boys were still yelling, and I stopped to listen. They were excited. There was no doubt of that, but somehow I could not imagine that they would yell in exactly that manner if one of them had been taken by a lion.

But now they seemed to be returning, and now and then it seemed to me that I could detect almost a note of merriment in their voices. I finally decided that there could be no doubt about it. There certainly had been no tragedy, though what had happened was still beyond us.

They came yelling back to camp where, by now, we had a camp light burning, and it was then that we learned what had occurred.

The boys, as I have explained, slept on tanned skins beneath a shelter, and one of them, who was so unfortunate as to be on the outside, had suddenly been awakened by having his tanned skin pulled abruptly from beneath him. He awoke suddenly, of course, and found himself staring directly into the face of a hyena. Hence his yell.

The hyena, with the skin in his mouth, naturally beat a very hasty retreat, while the other boys, startled into wakefulness, began to yell even before they knew just what had taken place. A word or two, however, from their despoiled companion made the matter entirely clear to them, and all in a moment they took out after the robber, yelling as they went. They recovered the skin, too, and appeared to enjoy the matter hugely. To Osa, Fritz, and me, however, the affair was not so humorous. The lion of our imagination had seemed so very, very real.

It was only a day or two after the hyena experience that we began to break camp. Our "vacation" had been a strenuous one, but we were happy. We had planned to do very little in the thorn bush country. Instead, we had had the good luck to accomplish a great deal. But that has often been our luck before, and my own belief is that that is one of the principal things that makes our work so fascinating. Still, it is not only our work that is interesting. Camping is interesting in itself.

There in the thorn bush country we usually returned to camp tired, hungry, thorn-scratched, and bitten by ants. We were always happy, of course, after a successful day with the wild animals, but almost every day was successful from that point of view. But as the sun slid down toward the horizon, and we made our way back to camp, Wah, our gibbon ape, would catch sight of us and come running to meet us, his long arms outstretched to balance himself, his long legs scurrying knock-kneed across the ground. He would throw himself on the first person he came to and laugh like a child, so glad was he to see us after we had been away all day. Then the four baby cheetahs would come rushing out and playfully grab us by the trousers and jump around stiff-legged like puppy dogs, anxious for us to play with them. This would generally make Wah jealous and he would go after one. The other three would pile on, and a free-for-all fight would start—not a vicious fight, for they were all friends, but a wooling match—and the cheetahs would always win, whereupon Wah would come and jump on someone's shoulder for protection.

On arriving in camp hot tea and biscuits were always ready, for the tent boys and cook would see us coming from a distance. After a cup or two of tea we would go to our tent, have a warm bath that would be waiting, change our clothes, and suddenly find that we were no longer tired. Instead, we almost invariably felt like a million dollars. Osa would then go to the cook and supervise dinner, while I would start unloading and loading plates and films in preparation for the morrow's work. Fritz would collect the guns and see that Orangi cleaned them properly, for on safari every gun is cleaned every evening whether it has been fired or not. They are then greased for the night, and each morning the grease is wiped out and the guns made ready for the day's work.

Four guns were always loaded and ready. Fritz, Osa, and I always kept our rifles on small pieces of canvas at the sides of our beds. Beside each gun we kept a flashlight, so that we might be ready for any prowling animal that might stray into camp during the night. Natives, of course, are not allowed to have firearms, but we always allowed Orangi to have one at night. He understood guns, and while he was not a good shot, he was fearless and could use a rifle, should any big animal get close to the boys' quarters.

Camping really need not be a hardship. Our camps are always comfortable and our meals are always good. Contrary to what most people think, we live really well. Such dinners as we usually have in camp are far rarer at home. We generally have a cocktail or a whiskey and soda, for instance, with a hors d'œuvres of caviar, anchovies, stuffed eggs, or a delicious paste that Osa makes of chopped sardines mixed with spices. Then a soup of bird, fish, or antelope meat. Next an antelope roast, perhaps, or broiled or fried steaks or birds or fish. We always have tinned vegetables, of course, but sometimes we find wild asparagus or mushrooms or spinach during the day. We always carry potatoes and onions, for they will generally keep for the length of the average safari if they are spread out in the shade every few days to keep them from molding. Before we leave on safari Osa buys fresh butter and mixes in salt until it is about half salt and half butter. When it is needed she merely washes out the salt. In addition to this we carry a very fine brand of tinned butter. For breads, pancakes, and cakes she carries prepared flours that we have had packed in sterile one-pound tins in America. This flour keeps almost forever, and is prepared in such a way that only the addition of water or tinned milk is necessary to make excellent biscuits, bread, or muffins on short notice. For desserts we have all the tinned fruits, while Osa is expert at making puddings and pies with ostrich eggs or dried egg powder. And there are other dishes galore. From this it will be seen that we live well, and have a wide variety of excellent foodstuffs.

After dinner we usually sit around the campfire, talking over the events of the day or the plans for the morrow, and stopping, now and then, to listen to the interesting wild animal sounds of the night—a lion roaring in the distance, hyenas howling or laughing, jackals yapping, a leopard grunting. Night birds are always about. Monkeys and baboons may be quarreling not far off as they settle in the trees for the night, and sometimes away in the distance we hear the trumpeting of elephants, while always, at the far end of camp, about their own campfires, the boys laugh and talk about the adventures of the day. Gradually the boys quiet down. Orangi comes to me, salutes, and asks "Shauri-a-Kesho?" Literally translated, this means "Business of Tomorrow," but what he means is "What are my orders for tomorrow?" I tell him the plans, he salutes again, and returns to his tent.

Then we turn in, and how good our air mattress beds feel. It seems as if I have no more than drawn the covers over me before I am sound asleep—no dreams, no tossing around, a good, sound, undisturbed sleep (unless some animal comes into camp)—and at four in the morning Suku, our tent boy, awakens us. In a jiffy we are out of bed, wide awake as our feet touch the ground, with no grogginess such as we have in the stuffy rooms of civilization—none of that dopey feeling of cobwebs in our brains. Our minds are clear, our muscles are fit, and we are anxious to get out for the adventures of the day. We awake to every new day with a feeling that all is well with ourselves and with the world.

Much has been written about the unhealthy tropics. I have never found them so. If proper precautions are taken with food, water, exercise, and the simple medical remedies with which to ward off malaria and a few other preventable diseases, I thoroughly believe that a person would live longer, and would be healthier and happier, on safari than in civilization.

9

WE HAD planned, even before we left America, to pay a visit, at some time during the progress of our aerial safari, to the pygmies who dwell in the vast Ituri Forest, deep in the Belgian Congo. Ten years or so before, Osa and I had had an opportunity to see some of these fascinating little people, and three years ago we made a motion picture called "Congorilla," a large part of which was taken in the Ituri Forest. We had learned a bit about the pygmies, consequently, and because we liked them we wanted to visit them again. And now, having returned to Nairobi from the thorn bush country, we decided that we would do as we had hoped for so long to do. We would not be able, unfortunately, to spend any great amount of time in the Ituri, for the rains were due to start soon, and we had urgent work to accomplish on the slopes of Mt. Kilimanjaro besides.

The great forest in which the pygmies live lies to the west of Lake Albert, which forms a part of the border between Uganda and the Belgian Congo. All of 25,000 square miles are included in this gigantic jungle, and though in recent years the Belgian Government has built roads here and there, has set up local headquarters for government representatives, and has otherwise moved to bring this region under control, still there are great sections that have never been visited by white men.

Stanley discovered this extraordinary forest, and it is sometimes called by his name. Sometimes, too, it is called the Congo Forest, or the Pygmy Forest, but more and more it is becoming known by the name of a river that flows through it—the Ituri. It is the largest remaining fragment of the immense forest which at one time seems to have covered the whole of equatorial Africa, and many are the fascinating stories that are told of it.

By the banks of certain rivers that traverse the Ituri Forest are sometimes to be found the "gallery formations," and when one comes upon these, one sees, in what otherwise might appear to be an "impenetrable" forest, great avenues of trees "like the colonnades of an Egyptian temple," which, as Schweinfurth says, are "veiled in leafy shade, and open into aisles and corridors musical with many a murmuring fount."

It was, then, to this district that we planned to go, and because gasoline could not possibly be obtained there, it was necessary that we send a supply ahead. A landing field, too, had to be prepared for us, and the "preparatory expedition" that we sent ahead had, in this case, to be given an unusually long time in which to prepare for our coming.

Weeks before we left, therefore, Bob Moreno and Fritz Malewsky had to be sent ahead by motor car, boat, and on foot, and long months before they started I had paved the

A KIKUYU VILLAGE. A Kikuyu village photographed from the air. These natives cut young saplings from the forest and use them to make a fence around their manyettas. The saplings take root and form a good protection from prowling wild animals.

ELEPHANTS FEEDING. Movie enlargement. This fine old bull and young female elephant were feeding on a ledge above the Victoria Nile. It was interesting to note that when we came along in our canoe, they did not lose their heads and stampede away. Instead they carefully felt their way directly toward us, swam around a small muddy space, and disappeared up a trail. This was a feat of memory, for it was their only way of escape and they had remembered it.

way for them by obtaining the necessary permits from the Belgian Government, and by interesting officials in our plans. One can readily see from this that wandering about Africa by air is not to be accomplished without preparations made in advance. Finally, however, the time came for Osa, Vern, and me to take off. Long since, Bob and Fritz must have entered the Belgian Congo, and we could only hope that, by now, they had been able to prepare a landing place for us near the spot that we had directed them to find.

The morning on which we started was beautifully bright, and once we were clear of the Nairobi field, Vern set his course a little to the north of west, with Entebbe, on the northern shore of Lake Victoria, as our first stopping place, and with the Belgian Congo border two hundred miles or so beyond.

It is difficult, when one is able to make such journeys by air, to realize that only forty-eight years ago Stanley was truthfully writing of the very district that we planned to visit that "for 160 days we marched through the forest, bush, and jungle without ever having seen a bit of greensward of the size of a cottage chamber floor. Nothing but miles and miles, endless miles of forest." Starvation, fever, and the hostility of natives were daily incidents of this terrible march, and during its disheartening length Stanley lost fully half his men, before, at last, he reached Lake Albert.

And here we were, at Entebbe, four hours or a little more from Nairobi! Stanley, in order to make his way into the region we were going to visit, was forced to create what almost amounted to an army, in order to overcome the fearful difficulties of the way, and here were we flying it in a few hours, and in the utmost comfort. In place of an "army" of hundreds upon hundreds of natives, Osa and I had with us only Vern Carstens, Helen Joyce, my secretary, who had recently come out from New York in order to dig me out from under the accumulation of details that had begun to swamp me, and a couple of our "boys." And now, after only one "hop" from Nairobi, Lake Albert and the edge of the Ituri were a mere two or three hours by air away. It is no wonder that it is a temptation to say that even Africa has changed, for most certainly it has.

We spent the night very comfortably at Entebbe, and early the next morning took off for Lake Albert. Diagonally across Uganda we flew, over beautiful, rolling country dotted with innumerable Buganda villages, and presently sighted the sparkling waters of Lake Albert ahead. Out over the lake Vern took the plane and finally, at its northern end, he set the ship down, taxiing up to the shore at the little Belgian government station of Mahagi. Hundreds of excited natives came running down to meet us, and when we stepped ashore one lone and much excited Belgian official greeted us in French.

None of us, however, could speak French, and the official could speak no English. Nevertheless, in an hour all our papers had passed his inspection, had been visaed and stamped and recorded and fixed up, and we, intent on the Ituri Forest, climbed into our plane once more, taxied out

in the lake and made a rough take-off, for the waves were
high.

Now, for two more hours, we flew over the northern part
of the Ituri Forest—the very forest through which Stanley
had struggled for 160 days. Now and then below us we
could see herds of elephants. Here and there, in tiny little
clearings, we sighted native villages. We flew low over one,
and the savages ran fearfully to cover like any flock of
frightened chickens. Farther on a herd of buffalo set up a
cloud of dust that trailed behind them. An enormous flock
of tropical birds rose suddenly in our very path and Vern
was forced to bank and turn abruptly to avoid them.

Then, quite suddenly, the miracle!

Long since, we had chosen the tiny little settlement of
Gombari as our destination at the edge of the Ituri Forest.
It was to this spot that, weeks before, we had sent Bob and
Fritz. We had a map, it is true, on which Gombari was
marked, but maps of such a region are of little value. Generally, in fact, they are a handicap, for rivers and lakes and
valleys that one can plainly see are all too commonly not
on the maps at all, while rivers and lakes and valleys that
have no counterpart in reality are often brazenly and vividly portrayed.

Thus Gombari, to us, was merely a point at the edge of
the Ituri Forest. We had all too few landmarks that would
help us find it. We had, as a matter of fact, expected to
hunt about more than a little before we located the place
at all, yet suddenly, directly ahead, we saw the grass roofs

that marked our destination. Here, I suspect, was a combination of excellent piloting on Vern's part, and a bit of luck besides.

We circled the village carefully, and presently made out the flags set up in a clearing to tell us where to land. Bob and Fritz, with the help of the local Belgian officials, had done their work well, and though the field was not extensive, it would serve. We circled about, now that we had found it, and made out Bob and Fritz with the Belgians as well and with I do not know how many hundreds of natives, all of whom were staring upward in amazement. Not a dozen people in the thousand or more who were waiting had ever seen an airplane before, and even the natives who had been told of the plane that was coming did not believe the story. The idea that white people would come flying out of the clouds was so perfectly preposterous. Still, they suspected that something unusual might happen, and so, from miles and miles around, they had gathered to see what it might prove to be.

We took another turn about the field, low, now, over the heads of the astounded gathering. The natives were leaping about in their excitement, raising their hands—pointing—shouting. Then, only half visible over at the edge of the forest, we spied another group. Down we flew, directly above their heads, and almost instantly they melted away among the trees. These were pygmies to whom the natives' grapevine telegraph had brought the news of our expected arrival. They had been curious, of course, and had come to see, but

FAREWELL DANCE OF THE TURKANA WOMEN. As we prepared to leave this good-natured tribe, the women danced around our big plane singing a chant that they had evidently composed for the occasion. All we could understand were the words "white man's bird." For some reason, the men did not join in.

THE WHITE RHINO. These two pictures, one of the white and the other of the black rhino, give a very good idea of their comparative shapes, if not sizes. The white rhino is much larger than the black. In this picture it will be noticed that the white rhino has a larger and longer head, a square mouth, is higher at the shoulder, and has a larger horn.

THE BLACK RHINO. The natures of the two rhinos are entirely different. The black rhino will quite often charge a human being while I have never known the white rhino to injure a human. The white rhino may be a shade lighter in color, but he is not white. Probably he got the name because he likes to roll in the alkali dust after he has been in the water. This dust dries on him and gives him a whitish appearance when seen from some angles.

they were frightened when the giant bird flew so low above them, and instantly fled.

Once more we circled the field before we landed. Across its none too perfect surface we bumped and rolled. We turned about and started to taxi back, but the shouting, screaming crowd was all about us. Bob and Fritz were frantically trying to drive the natives from our path, but to no purpose. For a minute or two it looked as if some of them would certainly be mangled by the propellers. But presently Vern gave up and stopped the motors. The danger of taxiing the plane any further through that uncontrollable throng was far too great.

But merely stopping was not enough. The horde of puzzled and curious natives attempted to swarm all over the plane, and for an hour or more we were hard put to it to keep them off. It was not that any of them intended to damage or steal a single thing. It was merely that so many curious hands could easily cause damage even without intending to.

At last, however, a godsend came to us in the shape of a heavy tropical downpour. The storm clouds gathered, the lightning flashed, and heavy peals of thunder boomed across our "flying field." Then the rain began to fall in great, soaking sheets, driving the natives off in scampering crowds, and leaving us to stake down the plane in comparative peace. Still, the rain failed to drive every native away, and, as we were engaged in making the plane safe, we suddenly

213

became conscious of the fact that a hesitant band of pygmies was tentatively approaching us from the forest.

Now these pygmies were the very creatures that we had come to see. Ten years before, Osa and I had been at this very spot. It had been for that reason that we had chosen to land here. And among the doubtful little group of diminutive natives that now approached so hesitantly we recognized several pygmies whom we had met on that visit ten years before. Furthermore, they recognized both Osa and me, and great was their rejoicing.

How long these tiny citizens of Ituri Forest have dwelt in its unmapped tangle not even the most learned scientist can tell. How they came there—why they still remain so small—what their development or lack of development has been no one has ever known. What we *do* know is that until the last six or eight years, they have been, so far as the average visitor to the Ituri Forest is concerned, hardly more than forest shadows, gone the very moment they become visible. But recently, what with the penetration of Belgian officials and the more numerous visits of explorers and scientists, at least a few of the pygmies who have had some opportunity to see and meet the strange big white men, have come to learn that no great danger to themselves lies in these strange creatures from a world the pygmy cannot even imagine. The result has been that slowly they have grown to be less timid—that they more readily show themselves—that some of them, at least, are willing of their own accord to come into the villages of the bigger natives in order to see and be seen by those of us who go there.

And now that the Gombari government station has been where it is for ten or a dozen years, they have learned that the white men who live there are really the friends of every pygmy of the whole Ituri Forest. Thus it is that they have overcome their fear of the whites and of the natives who live at the forest edge.

When Osa and I had visited Gombari before, these little people had been wild indeed, and we had been forced to go into the forest after them. But we had given them gifts— salt, for one thing—and so had made friends with them. Since then, too, they have learned that there is nothing to fear of anyone in Gombari. It was for all these reasons, to-gether with their insatiable curiosity, that they had hesi-tantly come out of the forest in the rain.

Their visit, however, was short, for the storm attained new proportions, which drove even the naked pygmies back into the forest and urged us to complete our task with the plane in order that we might take shelter in a three-room grass hut that had been assigned to us.

The rain came down in a veritable flood all that night and all the next day, keeping us to our hut, but giving us ample time in which to clean our cameras and lenses pre-paratory to photographing when the weather cleared.

All during the day natives, pretending to be on urgent business, made it a point to pass by our hut, each with a big banana leaf over his head to serve in lieu of an umbrella. They passed and repassed, in an attempt to satisfy their curiosity, nor did they worry unduly about the rain. Certainly their clothes did not suffer, for most of them had none.

But walking past the hut told them far too little, for we were hardly visible. Consequently, they began thinking up reasons for entering. One interesting old fellow appeared at the door with an old and mangy baboon, led by a bit of native rope and following his master as a dog might. Another appeared with a goat, several brought parrots, and a band of a dozen boys squatted under a tree beside our hut and played monotonously on small musical instruments made of pieces of wood to which bits of metal were attached. Oddly enough the youthful musicians managed, somehow, to entice somewhat weird and pleasing melodies from these odd affairs.

A woman who passed several times was so fat that she could hardly waddle along. It was funny to see her shapeless, black, and almost entirely nude figure as she wobbled from side to side, and we roared with laughter each time she appeared. She was not perturbed by our amusement, either, but laughed back at us with all the good-nature of an old southern "mammy."

The rain stopped finally, and early on the second morning after our arrival we were out on the flying field. It was a beautiful cloudless morning, but early as we had arisen, the pygmies were before us. A hundred or more of them were swarming about the plane when we appeared, and, as

A YOUNG SOMALI GIRL. The Somali are among the most intelligent
people in Africa, seldom having a permanent home, usually wandering
around the semi-desert country with their large herds of cattle, sheep, and
goats. Their hair is naturally straight and slightly wavy, but the girls twist
and braid it into strands.

THE MOST BEAUTIFUL MONKEYS. A troupe of Colobus monkeys, the most beautiful of the monkey family, with their long black and white hair and their benevolent faces. They are found throughout East and Central Africa, in the higher altitudes.

is the habit of pygmies, they were already periodically breaking into song and dance every few minutes.

When we arrived, the few among them who knew us ran up to greet us, though the others held back. However, I was soon distributing salt, which they gobbled down on the spot, and this brought the others up. In no time at all we were all friends, and what more joyous friends could one possibly have than such a group of pygmies. It almost seems as if, to them, there is no tomorrow and there never was a yesterday. Today is all that matters, or all that seems to. I wonder, sometimes, if their philosophy is so very far wrong.

All morning long we photographed that happy, dancing, singing throng. We made close-ups of the most interesting individuals. We had them dance their odd "snake" dance all about the plane. Incidentally, this long, undulating single file affair is no invention of enthusiastic American college students. For countless generations it has been the "highland fling" of the pygmies of the Ituri Forest.

By afternoon the ground had dried enough to make it possible to take off with the plane, and we decided to take some of these little people for a flight above their forest. The idea did not, at first, seem to appeal to them, and each one politely suggested that I take his next door neighbor. So fruitless was this method that we finally grabbed those nearest us, and thrust them into the cabin until it was almost full.

Now one of our particular friends among these tiny peo-

217

ple was a little chief who, with his wife, had met us ten years before. Both of them, it is true, flatly refused to be cajoled or pushed into the plane, but they had two little girls, about fourteen or fifteen years of age who, as tiny little creatures, we also remembered from our earlier visit. These girls were now quite grown up, were very intelligent indeed and were, I must say, quite the nicest-looking pair in the whole aggregation.

I decided that they at least, if not their parents, should go with us, and both of them were entirely willing. It took some time, however, to obtain the consent of their parents. Finally, however, I managed it, boosted the two little girls into the plane and climbed in after them. I closed the door, tried to get some order among the happy, chattering throng, and gave Vern the signal to go.

I will never forget that howling, singing, chattering group of little savages. They gathered about the windows, they swarmed over Osa and Vern, and they climbed into my lap. They pointed and yelled when they looked down on a river that they knew. The only trouble was that in order to keep from being half overcome by their odor we had to keep some of the windows open.

We flew out over the forest, and in fifteen minutes banked and turned about a hill they knew. Instantly they recognized it, and great was their amazement, for periodically they visited that hill in order, I gathered, to collect herbs, and it had always theretofore taken them days of travel to reach it.

Over African Jungles

We had, of course, taken many natives into the air during the past eighteen months. Some of them had been our "boys" from Nairobi, too—boys who had had many opportunities to learn something of the white man's marvels. Yet not once had any one of all the others we had taken up seemed for a moment to grasp the significance or appreciate the advantages of an airplane the way those happy little pygmies all seemed to do.

We flew about for an hour, and then landed, and as the enthusiastic little creatures jumped from the plane we counted them. Thirty-six, there were, who had taken that ride—thirty-nine with ourselves. Surely quite a number of individuals to go for a flight in a "ten place" plane.

But now that we had returned and had landed with a rush and a swoop, I learned something new about savages. So interested had I been in the reactions of the pygmies in the plane that I had given no thought whatever to the reactions of those we had left behind, but when, having landed, we opened the door and turned loose our thirty-six happy and excited little guests, I was amazed to see the chief's wife—the mother of the two little girls we had taken—run fearfully forward. She sought out her children and hugged them. She chattered and wept and kissed them repeatedly, fondling them and patting them, eager to reassure herself that they were safe and sound and whole.

Never before had I seen natives kiss each other. Never before, in twenty years spent largely among such people, had I seen such obvious signs of affection. That natives almost always treat their children well I knew perfectly, but not until that moment had I given a thought to the frightened mother who had seen her children disappear into the interior of the huge and noisy plane—had seen the thing sweep away with a roar—had seen it mount into the heavens and disappear so quickly beyond the horizon. What her fears were no one can imagine. She knew nothing of the possibility of engine failure or of conceivable airplane tragedies. Yet certainly she had been afraid—so much afraid, in fact, that in her relief at seeing them safe and sound once more, she showed all too plainly that mother love among the pygmies of the Ituri is no different from the mother love to which we have grown accustomed here at home.

But now it began to rain again. We were afraid that the seasonal rains were on, and were also afraid that the ground would grow so soft that we could not take off. Consequently, a few days later, when it had not rained at all the preceding night, we made a muddy take-off for our return journey.

Out over the Ituri Forest we flew, down so low that we only comfortably missed the tree tops and, I have no doubt, frightened the natives half out of their wits each time we passed a village in a clearing. In three hours, however (think of Stanley's 160 days), we were over Murchison Falls on the Victoria Nile. Below us a big bull elephant on a marshy little island splashed ashore. Hippo hurried from the marsh grass into the protection of the river. Thousands of crocodiles slid hurriedly from their resting places on the banks and disappeared beneath the surface of the water. A herd of seven elephants stampeded from the water's edge, and other herds rushed off into the trees.

We circled over beautiful Murchison Falls and flew up and down over the deep canyon through which the river runs. We saw other herds of elephants—a herd of buffalo—countless head of other game—and slept that night at Entebbe. Next day, so simply and so rapidly can one travel by plane, we were back at our home in Nairobi, none of us a whit the worse for a 2500-mile trip into the very heart of "wildest" Africa.

And now we set about preparing for a final aerial safari before making ready to return to America. Already we had a more than usually complete series of animal photographs, yet we knew, from experience, that one never is able to get too much. It was for this reason that we planned to visit a region new to us, but in which the game is as varied and as fascinating, I venture to say, as it is in any place in Africa. We wanted more photographs of lions, rhinos, elephant, buffalo, and leopard. That we were likely to get all these in one place was doubtful, of course, yet the spot that we had chosen held them all, and with luck we might succeed.

It is only natural that many of the people I meet after returning from Africa should ask questions about animals. The difficulty lies in giving answers. How easy it is to generalize, and thereby to go astray.

"What," someone may ask, "will a lion do if—?" Or

it may be that they will ask about a rhino or elephant or something else.

Now the truth, of course, is that while any of these animals have characteristics that long observation make reasonably clear, they are not invariably likely to react identically. If my questioners should ask themselves such a question as "What would a man do—?" they would immediately ask, "Which particular man?"

And thus, at least to a considerable degree, the answer depends upon an individual animal's reactions. Obviously the defenseless animals are likely to be timid. But of the five animals of Africa that are said to be "the most dangerous"—that is, the elephant, lion, rhino, buffalo, and leopard —one just cannot be certain. In general they may do thus and so, but if one is wise he will forever remember that the individual that is near by at the moment may decide, for any of a number of reasons, or for no traceable reason at all, to react quite differently. And then again, one's own experience may cause one to believe that this or that animal is "the most dangerous." I, for instance, am inclined to put the leopard in that class, for I have had too many of them charge so unexpectedly, and though many other animals are more powerful, few are harder to stop in a charge than a leopard.

Osa, on the other hand, is quite willing to give the rhino the preëminent position, for she has been charged by them many, many times, and, in particular, has been forced, on a number of occasions, to drop her fishing rod and take to some tree or other because, all unexpectedly, some ugly-tempered rhino has come snorting toward her when she was being as inoffensive as she knew how to be.

Others, of course, will advance the theory that the elephant or the buffalo or the lion deserves this doubtful palm, but I, myself, do not really believe that a single one of these animals goes about looking for trouble. Why should they? And if they charge, as any of them may do, it is because they have been given the impression that danger threatens, or for some other reason that undoubtedly seems equally good to them.

But this, I suspect, does not really apply to the rhino. His is a special case.

It must, of course, be remembered that a rhino's vision is not of the best. On the other hand his hearing and his sense of smell are excellent. Furthermore, he has no real enemies but man, and his brain, unfortunately for him, is small and consequently he is not overly bright. As a result of all this, here is what happens.

He catches a scent or hears a sound. Either one, goodness knows, will arouse him. But his ears and his nose are not likely to tell him in detail just what the scent or sound mean, and he naturally wishes to know. Consequently, he comes snorting and puffing up to see.

Now during most of the many, many thousands of years during which there have been rhinos, that was a perfectly safe thing to do. If the scent or the sound originated with an elephant, or a buffalo, or another rhino, even the bleary-eyed fellow himself could see, before he had come too close, that that was the case and could—as he usually does—call his charge off. If, on the other hand, the object of his investigation proved to be almost anything else under the sun, what of it? Practically nothing has ever been able to do him harm—until recently. But, within the last fifty years or so, white men have been appearing in the rhino country, and white men carry guns which give this newcomer considerably more concentrated power for destruction than even a rhino has. And here is where the small brain comes in, for its limited capacity has not, as yet, permitted the rhino to learn how deadly a white man is likely to be. The result is that these investigating charges too often result in dead rhinos, and unless real steps are taken to protect the blundering old fellows, it may not be so very long before their name will be added to the lengthening list of extinct animals.

But here I am, though I know better, generalizing again. I have already said that it is dangerous, for each question about animal behavior really requires an answer so long and complicated as to be impractical outside the pages of a scientific treatise. And, I can assure you, even rhinos have their own individualities, as we learned when, after we had returned from the pygmy country, we went to the beautiful plains at the northern foot of Mt. Kilimanjaro.

This magnificent mountain—the greatest and the highest in all Africa—lies to the south of Nairobi a somewhat greater distance than Mt. Kenya lies to the north. Like

A MASAI WOMAN. This picture was taken on the slopes of Mt. Kilimanjaro. These women are probably the most elaborately dressed of any in Africa. The wire once put on is never taken off; it is obtained by the men who make long journeys to trading posts for it.

ON TOP OF THE AFRICAN WORLD. The peak of Mt. Kilimanjaro. It is estimated that the snow is over a hundred feet deep on top. Inside is a deep crater, also filled with snow. While making this picture, it was hard for me to breathe on account of the rarefied atmosphere, and so cold that my hands were stiff and my nose and ears nearly frozen.

Kenya, Kilimanjaro is an extinct volcano, though it has been extinct for a much shorter time, as is proved by the fact that though Kenya's crater has long since been eroded away, Kilimanjaro's still forms a vast pit—more than a mile wide and six hundred feet deep—in its snow-and-glacier-covered summit.

The major portion of the mountain—perhaps all of it—lies in Tanganyika Territory, but the slopes to the north, and the plateau from which the mountain rises, run well over the line into Kenya Colony, forming a region where game is almost as numerous, and certainly as varied, as on the Serengetti Plains themselves.

This region was, then, an important one for us, and we accordingly arranged to spend some time there. We sent our motor cars ahead, consequently, and when sufficient time had elapsed for the motor party to get to the spot we had decided on, to erect camp and prepare a flying field, Osa, Vern, and I took off with the planes. The country over which we passed was much like that which we had seen between Nairobi and the Serengetti Plains. We saw the usual amount of plains game, but were constantly being surprised at the number of rhino that were visible. Now Osa, for the reasons I have given, has no great love for rhino. It was because of that, I suppose, that when we were halfway to our destination Osa suddenly realized that, in an airplane, *she* could charge a rhino for a change. Here, in other words, was an opportunity to give a rhino or two a taste of their own medicine.

Down we swooped, therefore, at the very next rhino we saw—our motors roaring and the great spread of our wings creating I know not what kind of a picture in the rhino's sluggish mind. But if his mind was sluggish, his legs were not. He had only one thought, obviously, and that was to get as far away as possible, and as rapidly as he could, from the gigantic bird that seemed to be threatening him. The ground was muddy, too, from a heavy rain of the day and night before, but that did not seem to hinder the old fellow. He splashed through the mud like a battleship through a head sea, and long after we had passed him and climbed back to a respectable altitude again, we could see him with our glasses as he kept up his retreat.

We found the camp site without trouble, and on the newly laid-out flying field the signals told us that everything was ready for us. We landed at once, and found an overawed gathering of Masai natives who had wandered in to inspect the camp. The camp itself contained endless wonders for them, but the great and noisy bird that swept down onto the field, only to open and permit us to step out, was really too much for them to grasp.

We had arrived just in time for lunch, and after we had eaten we set out in a motor car to inspect the country, for despite our wanderings in this portion of the world, neither Osa nor I had ever been in this particular region before. Nor would we have come now had it not been that Al Klein, who had handled the Davisons' safari, had told us that in his estimation this was one of the finest game regions in all Africa.

How beautiful many sections of East Africa can be, and how beautiful this district was. At one time all the region about our camp had undoubtedly been a lake, but in the course of time the lake has gone, leaving a great expanse of territory that measures thirty by fifty miles or so. In the very heart of this our camp was nestled, at the edge of a magnificent grove of trees.

Here and there about this ancient lake bottom were smooth, white alkali pans, any one of which might make a perfect landing place for our planes. Elsewhere were swamps, filled with papyrus and tiger grass ten to twelve feet in height. About the swamps the trees grew thickly, and through them countless criss-crossed game trails led to the water. Springs, too, were to be found here and there, bubbling with clear, cool water, generally in the shade of palm trees, while short, thick grass surrounded them, spreading on and on wherever the trees shielded it somewhat from the sun.

Gray little monkeys with long tails were everywhere. Brightly colored birds were all about. Pelicans, flamingos, herons, cranes, ducks, geese, and scores of smaller birds were almost always in evidence. About the swamps were wallows made by hippo, buffalo, rhino, and elephant. Lion and leopard spoors were on almost every trail. And somehow the whole region, dotted with trees and swamps, beautiful with grass and springs, bright with sunlight in the open places, seemed for all the world like a gigantic and beautiful park, laid out by a master landscape architect, as indeed it was, for here was the handiwork of the greatest Landscape Architect of all.

We naturally went to work with our cameras at once, for no one could fail to be enthusiastic in such marvelous country. Within ten minutes, too, of the time we left camp with our photographic truck for the first time we came upon the biggest female rhino and the smallest baby rhino I have ever seen. The mother was a remarkably fine specimen—big and broad and powerful. Her horns, too, were wonderfully symmetrical, and the larger one was all of three feet long.

The two were asleep when we sighted them—or rather when we sighted the mother, for the baby was so tiny that we did not see him at first. He could hardly have been more than a few days old, and I must admit that I had not realized how tiny a really little rhino is. He was, I should say, not a bit over eighteen inches tall, while, beside the great bulk of his powerful mother, he looked even smaller.

We have seen many baby rhinos, though this one certainly was the youngest we had ever come across, and I never had thought of them as "cute." But this little fellow really was. His legs did not quite coördinate as he trotted beside his mother. His manner was most babyish, and the little round button on his nose that would, in time, become a dangerous horn, gave him a most humorous appearance.

I grabbed my camera the moment I saw them, of course, and exposed a few hurried feet of film. But they promptly

VERN ARRIVES WITH SUPPLIES. Vern Carstens arrives at our Ngroon camp, while I run up to get the latest news. We built these landing fields all over Africa, sometimes taking four hours and sometimes seven days. All the work was done by thirteen natives. Here in America I often hear that cities and towns can't afford to build airports.

A DAY'S CATCH OF TROUT. A day's catch of brown and rainbow trout in the clear, cool streams that flow down from Mt. Kenya. These streams are so full of fish that the fish have turned cannibal and eat one another. Fritz, standing between Verne and me, has lived in Africa for many years, and was one of the most valued members of our safari.

moved off into the bush through which we could not follow, and I obtained little enough in the way of pictures. The result was that all the time we remained in that vicinity I kept hoping that we would come upon them again, but we never did.

We moved on as soon as the mother and her baby had disappeared, and within a mile sighted two big bull rhinos grazing at the edge of a patch of bushes. We stopped at a distance of a hundred feet, and in the next few minutes I got some excellent pictures. Then, quite suddenly, they saw us or heard us or caught our scent, and instantly the pair of them broke into a furious charge.

I kept my camera going, of course, while Osa, who sat in the front seat, beside Vern Carstens, who was driving, held her gun ready. But quite suddenly both rhinos stopped their charge at a distance of thirty feet or so, snorted, pawed the ground, glared at us, and then, almost as if we had not been there at all, fell to grazing again.

Now here was something new. We had long known that rhinos are prone to abrupt changes of manner. But never before had we ever seen the beasts come charging so furiously, only to stop and go to grazing almost under our very noses. Still, it suited me all right, for the camera was still grinding out scores and scores of feet of film.

And then Osa reached back and touched me on the knee, pointing backward. I turned as quickly and as quietly as I could, and saw a female rhino coming toward us directly

229

from behind. I had hardly turned, too, when she let out a snort and broke into a charge.

Here, I thought, was a pretty kettle of fish. If she should come banging into the truck from the rear, it might readily set off the two bulls that were so close to us in front. Furthermore, I had no gun, and to get the female, Osa would have had to fire between my legs or uncomfortably close to them, and anyway, she had to keep an eye on the two other beasts.

What to do I did not know, but luckily the female suddenly stopped her charge, snorted, backed up a step or two, snorted again, and then carefully walked in a half circle right around us. This, I thought, was the most amazing thing I ever saw a rhino do. Certainly she caught our scent clearly. She could not have failed to do so. Yet, after she had interrupted her charge, she showed not the slightest sign of causing further trouble, despite the fact that she eyed us constantly. Really, it seemed as if these Kilimanjaro rhinos had gone to a different school, and unless they had never known the scent of white men or of motor cars I cannot even yet imagine why they acted as they did.

Naturally, with the first rhinos we ran into in this region acting in so inexplicable a manner, we laid it to their own individual temperaments, but before we left the country, similar things had happened so often that our notions about rhinos in general had to be radically revised.

Within a few days, too, we had an even more interesting experience with two of the powerful brutes.

Over African Jungles

We were out, as we were for so much of the time, cruising about in a motor car, when we saw two rhinos crossing a large alkali pan. They were at a considerable distance when we saw them first, so we stopped and watched them with our glasses. They would not stop, we realized, while they were in the center of that bare alkali patch, and in a moment we saw that they were on a well-worn trail that led toward a muddy wallow at the edge of a little swamp some distance away. Feeling certain that they were headed directly for the wallow, we started the car, cut quickly "across lots," and chose a point of vantage from which we could get some good pictures when they came up.

We waited there for twenty minutes, expecting to see the rhinos arrive at almost any time. The center of the alkali pan was devoid of any vegetation, so there was nothing to make them stop there, but our move had put us in a position that cut off our sight of the beasts until they had moved several hundred yards, and then, when they reappeared, we were very much surprised to see that something unusual was in progress.

The two turned out to be a male and a female, and most certainly they were busily engaged in playing some sort of elephantine game. Furthermore, they were so intent on their own affairs that they paid no attention whatever to us.

The female, it soon appeared, was playing the coy maiden, while the male, as is the way of males the world over, was permitting himself to be led about in any way his sweetheart desired. Surely a coy rhinoceros is a contra-

231

diction in terms. But a rhinoceros lover is as much so. Yet
there they were, coy maiden and gentle lover, as plain as
day.

They had reached the edge of the alkali pan by the time
we could see them from our new position, and the female
stopped as if to graze. The male, then, with little, short
goose steps, edged toward her in his gentlest manner, but
when he was within a few feet, she whirled about and
goose-stepped away for fifty feet or so. It is impossible to
convey the ridiculous atmosphere that was so definitely a
part of the picture, and my imagination really needed very
little urging to make it possible for me to see the gentle
damsel with her finger on her lips, with her eyes cast down,
and "Oh! You bold man!" upon her lips.

This extraordinary love scene kept up for almost half
an hour before our very eyes (and before our cameras, too,
for I was filming it all) when, in their coy cavorting, the
male maneuvered himself into a position a hundred feet or
so away, where he caught our scent. And quite suddenly
his deep interest in his love-making evaporated into thin
air. He let out one surprised snort, deserted his sweetheart,
and dashed off into the bushes with his tail in the air.

We naturally thought that the female would do the same,
but she didn't. It was almost as if she had not seen him go,
and she obviously seemed puzzled at this sudden termina-
tion of his love-making. But in a moment she saw us, and,
wonder of wonders, she renewed her lover-like tactics for

WARRIOR IN FULL REGALIA. A young Kikuyu. These people start life by tending small herds of calves, sheep, and goats. As they grow older, they herd larger bunches of their domestic animals, after which comes a period of about two years when they are warriors with nothing to do; then they select a mate and live a life of leisure, their wives doing all the work.

VIEW OF LUXOR. Luxor, with its ruins and fine hotels. Before this picture was made, we were flying at 8,000 and 9,000 feet where it was cool. Approaching the city, we nosed down and could feel the stifling hot air being pushed into our planes. But it was interesting to see the ancient cities of Egypt from the air.

all the world as if she took our motor car to be another rhino.

Now both Osa and I have had literally all kinds of experiences with rhinos, but to have our motor car suddenly made the object of a female rhino's adoration was a new one. Furthermore, this new love affair was not merely momentary. For fifteen minutes or more the coy creature tried to break the silent reserve of our motionless truck. Truly, she must never before have met with so little response on the part of any creature of her kind upon which she had let the light of her eyes shine.

But I'll give her credit. She was a determined minx. She coyly retreated and nothing happened. She paused and waltzed about awkwardly. She playfully cropped a mouthful of grass and tossed it to the breeze. She daintily goose-stepped toward us, unobtrusively coming closer than she had been when she had begun her unsuccessful retreat. And she did all this over and over again, coming closer and closer each time.

And then, quite suddenly, she caught our scent.

"Hell hath no fury," someone has written, "like a woman scorned."

And the same applies to rhinos.

With an angry, outraged snort the coyness dropped from the furious female. Down went her head. Up went her tail, and so suddenly as to amaze us, she charged headlong, and all in a moment crashed (luckily at an angle) against our fender.

But we were not the only ones to be surprised. The metallic clang that resulted from her charge, and our own shouts were new sounds to her ears. And, too, this iron-skinned boy friend with which she had been philandering had suddenly proved so utterly detestable. But now, having shown her hostility to the unutterable disdain with which she had been received, she snorted angrily again, and abruptly departed for the alkali pan at her top speed.

It was not long after this that Osa, who had for some time been less than usually energetic, became really ill, with the result that Vern and I flew with her at once to Nairobi where she was put in the hospital. The reports from the doctors, however, were entirely optimistic, and neither of us realized that this illness would ultimately be the cause of our return to America. The first reports, though, suggested nothing like that, and we were told that, for a time, she should rest from the energetic life we always live on safari. Consequently, leaving her comfortable and in good hands, Vern and I flew back to camp, after having arranged to have reports brought to us periodically by air.

The next few days after our return resulted in hundreds of feet of the best animal pictures I have ever taken, but as so often happens, the better the pictures the less exciting is the story of their being taken.

We had located, a few miles from camp, a beautiful open spot, thirty acres or so in extent, where animals were always numerous. The open space itself was almost flat, while dotted across it were little half-acre swamps filled with swamp grass and occasional palms. At one end, however, lay a much larger swamp, in the center of which stood a gigantic, wide-spreading tree.

We had visited the place several times, but on the day I particularly have in mind, the animals and birds were especially interesting. As we drove up to it scores of baboons swarmed up the trees and barked at us. A dozen or so wart hogs ran across our path, and within five minutes two rhinos made impressive charges which did not carry through.

A herd of ten beautiful lesser kudu wandered by, stopping to stare at us for a few minutes. A herd of giraffe clumsily headed toward us, detoured about the car, and rushed away along the trail by which we had come.

We drove up to the edge of the big swamp, and a few minutes after we had stopped the car and I had climbed up on top in order to look around, I saw two elephants—a full-grown female and an enormous bull—as they slowly made their way toward the swamp by a game trail a hundred yards or so away.

They seemed half asleep as they meandered along, but they did not pause until, after splashing through the shallow water of the swamp, they reached the shade of the big tree in its center. Here they stopped and seemed to go sound asleep, their only movement being the flapping of their huge ears as the flies bothered them.

Here, I thought, was an opportunity for a picture, and I decided not to let any of the other animals lead me away from those elephants. Consequently, I set up my cameras, and we made ourselves comfortable while we were waiting for the elephants to complete their siesta and return.

We sat there for hours, but without a monotonous moment. Far out in the swamp we could occasionally make out the movements of a herd of fifty or so buffalo. Two great shapes left the swamp on the opposite side, and with our glasses we could plainly see that they were hippopotami. Four half-grown cheetah ran across the opening behind us, and within a few minutes a rhino followed. Reedbuck appeared now and then, and seeing us, suddenly bounded away out of sight. Monkeys dropped down out of the trees and played in the grass, or, standing upright on their hind legs, stared at us before bounding back into the branches.

A big hornbill settled in a tree not far away and croaked complainingly. Vultures sat hunched in rows on a long dead branch, without in the least discouraging the multi-colored parrakeets, which flew swiftly from tree to tree, their odd sounds decidedly pleasant in contrast to the croaking hornbill, and their bright happiness contrasting sharply with the ghoulishness of the vultures.

But fascinating though all this was, I refused to try to photograph any of it for fear of missing the elephants when they should return. And then, after four hours of waiting, we saw the elephants shift their positions, saw them shake off the lethargy that had descended upon them, and saw them, worse luck, go shuffling deeper into the swamp until they disappeared from sight among the trees at its farther end.

So there went the object of our wait, and there was nothing to do but head back for camp. Only Vern and I were in the car, and Vern was driving, for I wanted to be ready with my camera in case anything should give me an opportunity for pictures. Vern started the motor, consequently, and we drove off, cruising slowly in and out, watching as we went.

We left the park, passed through a corner of the forest, passed the edge of an alkali pan, and saw, at the edge of a large clump of trees and bushes, a fine, maned lion and a beautiful lioness. We drove up to within a hundred and fifty feet and stopped, for the lion rose to his feet, snarled angrily, and stood looking at us while he lashed his tail furiously back and forth.

We waited for a few minutes and he calmed down a bit, but when we started the next move forward he was instantly at it again. We waited longer this time but when, on our next attempt to move, the lion seemed definitely angry and ready to charge, Vern stopped again.

"Go ahead!" I whispered. "Go ahead. Move up fifty feet or so."

But Vern did not agree.

"Have a heart, Martin," he objected. "I haven't any gun, and that lion looks bad."

"Go on," I insisted. "I've got a gun back here."

"Yes," grumbled Vern, "and you've got a camera, too. Your darned pictures mean too much to you, and I'm interested in my skin."

Still, he started the car and had moved forward thirty feet or so when the lion charged. I was working my camera for all I was worth when suddenly I was thrown almost off my feet as Vern swung the car about with a lurch and stepped on the accelerator. Off we went, careening and bumping while the lion, apparently with the idea, which was true, that he had frightened us off, stopped and snarled again.

Off went Vern for a couple of hundred yards. Then he stopped, and I must say he was angry.

"Go on back alone, you damn fool," he growled. "But I'll be hanged if I go with you, even if I have to walk to camp. There you are all protected back there. But what the devil would I do without a gun, out here in this open seat?"

He certainly laid me out in grand style, and, because I deserved it, I really could not say much in reply. We headed for camp, consequently, but I noticed that Vern never thereafter left his gun behind.

From our camp Mt. Kilimanjaro was a magnificent sight when the clouds that often hang about the mountain's hoary summit cleared away and gave us a view of its snow-covered crest. Often the great white arc of the summit seemed utterly cut off from the earth from which it rises, and seemed to float like some beautiful mirage high in the brilliant air.

We watched it at every opportunity, and finally, one perfect day, decided to make a flight about the peak, which rises 19,324 feet into the sky. Vast as Mt. Kenya is, Mt.

Over African Jungles

Kilimanjaro is more vast, and this greater mountain is higher as well—is, in fact, Africa's greatest.

We took off easily, and climbed rapidly until we struck the clouds. But with the increasing altitude we climbed more and more slowly until it seemed to me that we would never win through to the clear air above. But, fighting for every additional foot, Vern at last brought the big ship above the clouds, and there, glittering white in the vivid sunlight, the vast, snow-capped crest lay before us, with the brown rocks below the snow fields somber and dark in contrast.

All about the vast peak lay a deep collar of fleecy cloud, through which we had flown. We could not see the plains from which we had come, and Kilimanjaro looked like a great island, rising from that undulating sea of cloud.

Even over Kenya I had had no such sense of grandeur, and this, with the exhilaration caused by the altitude and the cold, gave me a new sense of the magnificence of Nature.

My instant desire was to fly over the summit, but Vern vetoed my notion. He knew, far better than I, the dangers that lurk over such a snow-covered peak where irresistible "down drafts" caused by the cold of the ice fields, might readily have sucked us down into the vast dead crater that lay behind those glacier-and-snow-covered walls.

All about the great crest we flew, and yet, so vast is this great peak, we had no feeling for the speed of our plane. Instead we seemed at times to be floating motionless in space—miles above the earth—thousands of miles from the world of men—viewing a world so untouched by anything

239

we knew that it was impossible not to feel that we were closer to the Maker of it all.

Neither Vern nor I felt much like talking up there with the marvelous beauty of the mountain close beside us, and even when we turned about and dipped down into the clouds once more we had no inclination to talk. Nor did we find words easy when we had landed and were once more in camp. Experiences such as that flight come rarely in this world, and are subjects, it seems to me, that are much too vast for words.

But our time there beside the great mountain was coming to an end. Osa was still in the hospital, and on one occasion I had received urgent word to come at once. It is true that I found her sitting up in bed and looking as bright and chipper as she had ever looked. But she had been ill the night before, and even the doctors began to admit—to me—that it might be better if she were under the care of the best physicians of England or America.

Furthermore, except for that, we had been wonderfully fortunate during the year and a half that we had spent with our planes in Africa. Thousands and thousands of feet of film had been developed, and in that collection, we felt sure, was material for the best picture of Africa that we had ever obtained. To cut it, however, to edit it, and to make it ready for "the silver screen" we must return to America.

I looked about the beautiful country that surrounded our camp. I looked up again at the snow-white crest of Kili-

THE FOUR OF US. We four, who finished the safari after the other had returned to America. Osa and I would sleep inside the plane while Vern and Bob slept under the wings. Osa cooked meals on a small portable gasoline stove. Our table was a tarpaulin on the ground; but we were happy and away from the turmoil of a troubled world.

ANCIENT EGYPTIAN TEMPLES. The temples of Abu Simbel were a magnificent sight from the air. Hour after hour, we floated over such ruins of a vanished civilization, and it was mightily impressive. In the midst of all this, we beheld modern Egypt going about its business of living along the Nile in the same manner as their ancestors.

manjaro. It was hard to bring myself to leave. But then, we could return.

The trucks were ready to carry our belongings back to Nairobi when Vern and I took off in the plane, but Kilimanjaro and the animals would remain. I was suddenly very glad of that, for the world to which we shortly must return is one that has been so "improved" by civilization that there is little left within it to compare with the perfection and the beauty of this wilderness we were leaving.

IO

THE field work of our expedition was over. Furthermore, the doctors had told me that while Osa was in no immediate danger, an operation was inevitable and that it would be well to get her to a specialist as soon as possible. This, of course, meant that we must return to America as quickly as we could.

Thus it was that I hurriedly developed the last of my film and wound up a thousand details. Vern overhauled the planes with more than usual care, working early and late. Endless packages of freight were prepared and sent off. Quantities of film and plates were packed with the greatest care and started on their way to New York.

But now came another problem.

We had decided to fly from Nairobi to England, there to take ship for America. At first that seemed a difficult task, for while Osa and I had licenses, neither of us had had enough hours in the air to give us the mastery of a plane that would be required for so prolonged and difficult an air journey. Anyway, Osa would not have been up to handling a plane, despite the fact that she could be made perfectly comfortable as a passenger.

Vern, of course, is a highly competent pilot, but our second plane required another. And then we learned that a friend of ours and a pilot of experience, Mostert by name, was planning to return to England with his wife. Having learned that we soon made an arrangement with him. He and his wife were to take our smaller plane, and in this way they got their trip to London while we were able to profit by their experience, for Mostert had flown this route before.

With this settled, it only remained for us to decide what to do with our pets. We had a fine tame leopard, Osa's four young cheetahs, Toto Tembo, a baby elephant, and a very docile and affectionate hyena. That hyena, I have found, requires more explaining than any of the others, for everyone thinks of these beasts as repulsive. This one, however, was anything but that. He was utterly devoid of the characteristic and objectionable hyena scent, and he had many of the characteristics of a faithful dog.

This menagerie stumped us for a while, but Helen Joyce, my secretary, agreed to oversee its journey to America. Of course, she had to have help, so we arranged to send a Meru boy named Twarugoji with her in order that he might play valet to the animals. Accordingly, we obtained the necessary permits from the Kenya Colony officials for both the boy and the animals, and after much red tape, finally completed the necessary arrangements with the East African and the United States governments, obtained passage from East Africa to New York for Miss Joyce, Twarugoji, and the animals, and now were ready to take off in our planes, with Wah, our pet gibbon, and Syksie, Vern Carstens' pet monkey, for London.

We made a bed for Osa in the larger of the two planes, surrounded her and raised her with pillows until she could see out the window, and after all our numerous good-bys were said, took off, dipped our wings to our waving friends, and headed toward Egypt. We were glad to get under way, of course, and glad that America was ahead, but East Africa has long been home for us, and we were sorry to leave our friends in the little city of the game fields—the most interesting little city, it seems to me, in all the world.

Out over the Kidong Valley we flew, and ran squarely into heavy clouds that closed in all about us. Vern circled and twisted, flew through holes, and turned again. But finally, gaining altitude, we climbed above the clouds and laid our course for Tororo in Uganda, where we stopped for gas. We ate lunch there, as well, and then took off for Juba, in the Sudan.

We flew for hours, and late that evening had still failed to locate Juba. On we flew, with the Nile below us, not knowing where our stopping place was. And then, ahead, I saw the village of Mongalla. I recognized it instantly, and knew that we had passed Juba. So back we flew, this time very low, passing many herds of elephants on the way. It was just after dark when we reached Juba and landed. Mostert and his wife were already there, of course, and were worrying about us, for we were hours overdue.

We were off at dawn, giving the Mosterts and the

VALLEY OF THE KINGS. A view from the air, made as we were leaving Luxor in Egypt. It was a hot and desolate place, and one wonders why the kings wished to be buried here. Not a blade of grass, not even a bush for miles about.

OVER THE PYRAMIDS. Airview of the Pyramids and the Sphinx in Cairo. This seemed like the end of our journey, for once more we were back to good hotels, cafés, theaters, and modern stores; but we still had a long trip ahead of us, west along the Mediterranean to Tripoli and Tunis, then across the water to Sardinia and Corsica, to France and through Europe to England.

smaller, slower plane, half an hour's start, only to find that we reached Malakal, in the horrible heat of the Sudan, shortly before they did. We ate lunch and gassed up, glad to take off and climb out of the infernal heat. At eight thousand feet we were comfortable again. In fact, Osa asked for a blanket with which she covered herself as she lay in bed reading, sleeping, looking out the window, or playing with Wah and Syksie.

That night we slept in Khartoum, and I could not help marveling at the day's trip. In ten hours we had covered a distance that had taken us seventeen days by Nile boat only a few years ago.

The following evening we stopped at Wadi Halfa, had cocktails with the governor and, worse luck, lost one of our passengers. Poor Syksie, while playing in the yard of the rest house just before dinner, was bitten by a snake and died that night.

We took off early the next morning, flew over the temple of Abu Simbel—passed more temples—more ancient ruins —circled Luxor and landed to spend the night at one of Cook's excellent hotels. Next day we visited the Valley of the Kings and particularly King Tut's tomb, and after another night at Luxor, made an early morning start for Cairo. We circled low over the Valley of the Kings in order that I might make movies, then headed downstream, passing over more and more ruins and temples until late in the afternoon, when we left the Nile and flew out over the silent, deserted waste of the desert of Egypt.

Over African Jungles

Up to this time we had followed the Nile, but now we were over the burning sand. The heat was terrific, and even a mile in the air was terribly oppressive. Vern took the ship higher, consequently, but not until we reached 10,000 feet was it possible for us to feel cool.

It was near nightfall when we circled the Pyramids and the Sphinx, looking down upon these venerable relics as the setting sun cast their long shadows across the sands. Then, in another few minutes, we landed at Cairo's sandy airdrome and were driven to our hotel.

The "wilds" of Africa were far behind us now, but we were half lost, nevertheless, in the jungle of red tape through which we had to hack our way. We remained in Cairo for a week, while we went about the complicated task of obtaining the necessary permits to fly over the Italian and French colonies in North Africa. We were told that we must seal our cameras, for we would fly near certain fortifications, pictures of which must not be taken (for fear, I suppose, that we would turn such pictures over to the United States Government for use when the Navy goes over to capture all this region).

It was a hard week, I must admit, but it passed. With our permits finally in order we took off, spending the first night at Mersa Matruh, the last city at the northwestern corner of Egypt. Here, as in every other stopping place from Nairobi to London, we had to fill out the usual blanks, telling, for the thousandth time, where our fathers were born, where we were born, what our citizenship was, etcetera, etcetera. But at Mersa Matruh, one question, at least, was downright original. It is hard to believe, but as Heaven is my witness, I was asked, "Have you any coffins aboard?"

We had watermelon for dinner that night, I remember. The desert came right down to the Mediterranean, leaving barely enough room for the little city, yet there was the watermelon, and a delicious one, too. As a matter of fact, it was so good that I bought a great big one to eat in the plane the next day. But watermelon for dinner did not offset the effect of the mosquitoes that night. They were terrible, and the hotel had no nets.

Next morning, covered with welts and red-eyed for want of sleep, we took off again, flying out over the desert in the stifling heat. Vern flew high, of course, in order that we might keep cool, but when, at Bengasi, he nosed the ship down, it was as if we were entering the door of a furnace.

Still, we had a good night's sleep at Bengasi, and early the next morning were off on our first water jump, which took us across the Gulf of Sidra, a great indentation in the coast of Libya. For nearly two hours we were out of sight of land, while steamships and sailing vessels passed constantly below us.

That afternoon we landed at Tripoli, where we had the pleasure of taking tea with Commander Balbo, the great Italian flyer who led the Italian planes across the Atlantic to the World's Fair at Chicago. He was most considerate of us, placing his motor cars at our disposal and offering the assistance of his air force. He even waived the usual landing fee, saying that he had been treated so generously in America that he was glad to try to repay flying Americans in kind.

Tripoli is a larger edition of Bengasi, as clean and beautiful a city as I have ever seen. It is beautifully parked, the buildings are handsome, almost every person is well dressed and seems prosperous, and the blue Mediterranean rolled in directly in front of our fine hotel. The hotel management gave us the best that was available, too, and even Wah had a room to himself.

On the following day we took off on our second water jump, and we spent that night in Tunis. The city reminds me somewhat of Marseilles—it is French, of course—but coming up to the city we had to fly a very complicated course. First we approached the city to a certain mark. Here we had been instructed to turn out to sea. Then, once clear of the coast, we turned and entered the mouth of the bay, turned again at another point, and so found our way to the airdrome. And who, in the name of Heaven, wants to see their old fortification anyway?

We remained a day in Tunis in order to give Vern a chance to check his engines before the long Mediterranean crossing, but on the morning of the next day we were off again. It was a beautiful day, and in a very little while we were out of sight of land. Shortly, however, haze began to gather, and before long we could not see the horizon. I was at the wheel at the time, and in no time at all I was completely bewildered. Vern just sat and grinned at me

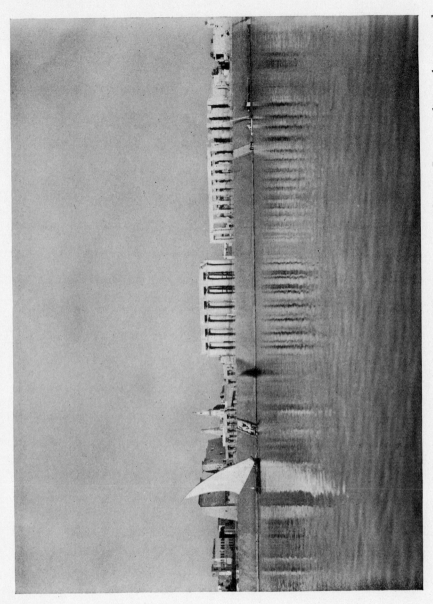

TEMPLES OF THE NILE. These ancient temples are on the Nile at Luxor, a lazy, sleepy, and most interesting spot. Unfortunately, we were here in the hottest season when it is a real effort to move around.

FLYING INTO A STORM. The "Spirit of Africa" flying into a storm. Our planes, being amphibians, were a great comfort to us when we were flying over rocky country in the vicinity of large bodies of water. At such times, we would raise the wheels in readiness for an emergency landing.

until I was so hopelessly lost that I had to turn the wheel over to him. On we flew, still with nothing that would have helped me find my way, and finally—it seemed a miracle to me—we sighted Cagliari, the capital of Sardinia, ahead, not more than a mile off our course.

We landed at the military airport, where the Italians again did everything they could to help us. Then, after a light lunch, we took off again, flew the length of Sardinia, crossed the strait that separates the island from Corsica, followed the beautiful shore line of that lovely island, and after three more hours over the sea, Vern set us down—another miracle—at the Cannes airport.

Now the eternal feminine stepped in, and we spent the next day at Cannes so that Osa could visit the hairdresser. However, the next day we took off across the magnificent Maritime Alps. It is a lovely country at any time, but we were flying across it in July, when everything was green and beautiful.

We stopped at Lyons for lunch, and taking off again, landed at Le Bourget in the late afternoon. Now, however, we were in Paris, and again the feminine asserted itself. We waited two days, consequently, while Osa purchased the dresses that were so vital in her scheme of things. Then we were off to London, where we were met at the airport by a host of friends.

Delay, by now, was no longer on our schedule. We made arrangements to ship our planes to New York on the S.S. "Manhattan." At Southampton, consequently, they were taken apart, were stowed on the deck of the big ship, and six days after we arrived in England, we were at sea.

What a year and a half that was!

We had flown for sixty thousand miles over Africa and Europe, without an accident that is even remotely worthy of the name. Surely, that is a recommendation for those marvelous planes of ours, as it certainly is for Vern Carstens.

And our pictures. Never before, in twenty years of photography, had we brought home pictures more unusual, and never, in all our work in the fields, had we had so carefree a time—so thrilling a feeling of absolute freedom.

And now that our picture "Baboona" is completed—now that all the endless details that go with such a task are drawing to a close—we are planning again. Even Wah, I do not doubt, is hoping that he will soon start another aerial safari. And we intend to. Osa has completed a long siege in the hospital, and now is as fit as she ever has been. Our pets, aside from Wah, have been put in the St. Louis Zoo, where you may call and see them.

And already we have made our plans to visit Borneo, to search for elephants, for the elusive hairy rhino, for the myriads of jungle game, and the Tengerra head-hunters.

But just because our next trip is to take us off to Borneo, don't think that Africa does not still call us, for it does. We have plans for more trips there, and others to still other portions of the world. In fact, Osa tells me that the safaris we have planned will require a hundred years. After that, we don't know what we will do.

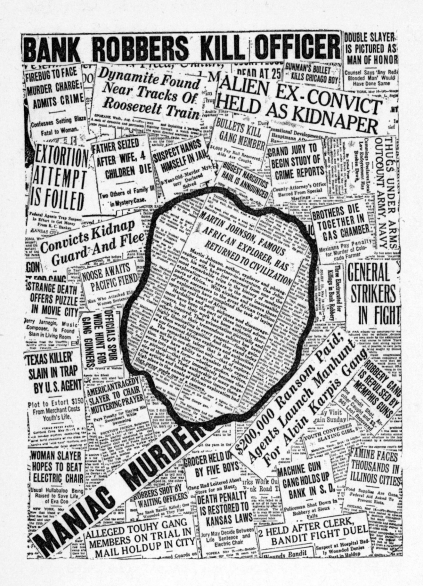

BANK ROBBERS KILL OFFICER

DOUBLE SLAYER
IS PICTURED AS
MAN OF HONOR

Counsel Says 'Any Red
Blooded Man' Would
Have Done Same

FIREBUG TO FACE
MURDER CHARGE;
ADMITS CRIME

Confesses Setting Blaze
Fatal to Woman.

*Dynamite Found
Near Tracks Of
Roosevelt Train*

DEAD AT 25

GUNMAN'S BULLET
KILLS CHICAGO BOY

**ALIEN EX-CONVICT
HELD AS KIDNAPER**

BULLETS KILL
GANG MEMBER

$4,000 Pay Roll Recovered;
Aids Are Caught.

FATHER SEIZED
AFTER WIFE, 4
CHILDREN DIE

Two Others of Family Ill
in Mystery Case.

SUSPECT HANGS
HIMSELF IN JAIL

6-Year-Old Murder Mys-
tery Declared
Solved

GRAND JURY TO
BEGIN STUDY OF
CRIME REPORTS

County Attorney's Office
Barred From Special
Meetings

THUGS UNDER ARMS;
OUTCOUNT ARMY NAVY

**EXTORTION
ATTEMPT
IS FOILED**

Federal Agents Trap Suspect
in Effort to Get Money
From K. C. Banker.

KANSAS CITY

Convicts Kidnap
Guard And Flee

BIGGEST NARCOTICS
HAUL IS ANNOUNCED

BROTHERS DIE
TOGETHER IN
GAS CHAMBER

Mexicans Pay Penalty
for Murder of Colo-
rado Farmer

NOOSE AWAITS
PACIFIC FIEND

Man Who Attacked Eld
Woman Sentenced

STRANGE DEATH
OFFERS PUZZLE
IN MOVIE CITY

Jerry Jarnegin, Music
Composer, Is Found
Slain in Living Room

MARTIN JOHNSON, FAMOUS
AFRICAN EXPLORER, HAS
RETURNED TO CIVILIZATION

Three Electrocuted for
Killings in Bank Robbery

GENERAL
STRIKERS
IN FIGHT

OFFICIALS SPUR
WIDE HUNT FOR
GANG GUNNERS

**'TEXAS KILLER'
SLAIN IN TRAP
BY U.S. AGENT**

Plot to Extort $150
From Merchant Costs
Youth's Life.

AMERICAN TRAGEDY
SLAYER TO CHAIR
MUTTERING PRAYER

Pays Penalty for Slaying His
Sweetheart While
Swimming

ROBBERY GANG
IS REPULSED BY
MEMPHIS GUNS

$200,000 Ransom Paid;
Agents Launch Manhunt
For Alvin Karpis Gang

YOUTH CONFESSES
SLAYING GIRL

**WOMAN SLAYER
HOPES TO BEAT
ELECTRIC CHAIR**

Usual Hullabaloo Being
Raised to Save Life
of Eva Coo

GROCER HELD UP
BY FIVE BOYS

Gang Had Loitered About
Store for an Hour.

DEATH PENALTY
IS RESTORED TO
KANSAS LAWS

Jury May Decide Between
Life Sentence and
Electric Chair

MACHINE GUN
GANG HOLDS UP
BANK IN S.D.

Policeman Shot Down in
Robbery at Sioux
Falls

FAMINE FACES
THOUSANDS IN
ILLINOIS CITIES

Food Supplies Are Gone,
Federal Aid Asked To
Prevent Riots.

MANIAC MURDER

ROBBERS SHOT BY
WAITING OFFICERS

ALLEGED TOUHY GANG
MEMBERS ON TRIAL IN
MAIL HOLDUP IN CITY

2 HELD AFTER CLERK,
BANDIT FIGHT DUEL

Suspect at Hospital Bad-
ly Wounded Denies
Part in Holdup

Appendix: Photographic Equipment

ONCE before I wrote a chapter on tropical and big game photography, but since then conditions have undergone a change. New types of cameras have been developed, of course, but more important than that have been the changes in sensitized emulsions, bringing about a change in the type of cameras that can now be used to the greatest advantage.

In this chapter I shall deal with the equipment that I think best for use by the amateur and the more advanced amateur who has been successful in photography in the temperate zones. Professional photographers, of course, need no advice except, perhaps, a few hints which may help them in case they have had no experience in photographing wild game.

I wish it understood that in recommending photographic apparatus, I am not doing so because of any affiliation with manufacturers. Neither do I receive any pay or compensation whatsoever. Certain apparatus has given me my best results and has taught me which type is best suited for my special uses. It is this information that I feel free to pass on.

I shall pass over the moving picture cameras quickly. Nearly every traveler now uses the 16 mm. size and I have seen some remarkably fine movies made with them. I recommend that those wishing to photograph wild animals carry three-, four-, and six-inch lenses, and of no longer focal length than the six-inch unless well advanced in photographic work. With a six-inch 16 mm. lens you will be able to photograph any species of game if you have patience. Be sure you have a good steady tripod for any lens longer than a two-inch, and, *for Heaven's sake, make your panoramic scenes slowly!* I have seen so many good scenes ruined by fast "panning"; pan just as slowly as you can, and play safe.

As for the kind of cameras—I have seen fine results with both the Bell & Howell Filmo and the Eastman Ciné-Kodak. If you can afford it, use the new Eastman Ciné-Kodak Special. I have just completed some experiments with this wonderful deluxe machine and can thoroughly recommend it. It will do everything any professional camera will do—fade-outs, dissolves, variable speed, double lens turret, double exposure, lap dissolves, slow motion, etc.—it is really a most remarkable bit of precision.

To those who wish to use the 35 mm. I recommend the Bell & Howell Eyemo with 47 mm. 3-¾, six-inch lens. I own twelve of these cameras and use them every day, for they have the advantage of being quickly set up and easily operated. Incidentally, they are ideal for aerial work.

For professional cameras I use Bell & Howell and Wall Sound Cameras, all motor driven.

Now the type of film you use depends on how far afield you are going. If you are in contact with a laboratory where you can have your film developed not more than two months after exposure, then you may use Super-sensitive Panchromatic or Super X Panchromatic and get wonderful results;

but if you have a long safari that takes you into damp forests or if you are out during the rainy season, then use regular Par Speed Orthochromatic and play safe. With Super-
sensitive Panchromatic or Super X Panchromatic you will
get fine results if weather conditions are right and you can
develop soon after exposure. But with the slower Par Speed
Orthochromatic emulsion you can take liberties in wet
weather or damp forests that would not prove successful
with the other emulsions. Whatever you do, decide on one
emulsion and stick to it. In the big game country you will
get wonderful opportunities for most interesting pictures,
but the opportunities may come without warning. Because
of that, try to get a *good* picture and do not experiment to
get a *better* picture, for wild jungle dwellers do not pose
for re-takes. Catch them while you can.

The big game country is unexcelled for color photography
and as a rule the light on the plains is good for this work.
I wish the 16 mm. photographers would not rush through
Africa as most of them do. I cannot imagine anything more
beautiful or better adapted for color work than the scenes
from a blind at a waterhole. But this requires time and
patience. The waterhole country is generally off the beaten
path. Building blinds and waiting for the game to get used
to them takes time, but the results will be marvelous. Imagine zebra, giraffe, ostrich, and the wide range of antelope
in color.

A new development in color work has just been brought
out, which is known as Kodachrome. Kodachrome does not

require a filter in making or projection, but can be used with the same ease and under the same conditions as black and white, except that the operator must bear in mind that Kodachrome requires the next larger diaphragm opening than is recommended for Panchromatic films. This means that the film can be used in any camera taking 100-foot rolls of film, regardless of the lens equipment, opening an entirely new field for color photography.

Now, to still cameras. By all means take a Kodak using roll film, and be sure to carry a portrait attachment for getting native shots.

MINIATURE CAMERAS

Personally, I never use a camera smaller than 2¼" x 2½", although some of my friends do. Out in Nairobi I had a very complete laboratory and developed many rolls of "Minnie" film for my friends. (The term "Minnie" is usually used to designate any negative 1-⅝" x 2½" or smaller.) I found that only a small percentage of their pictures were suitable for enlargement, but the fact that these little cameras allow thirty or more exposures to each loading, and that the cost is very small, allows the owner to make so many negatives that he can experiment in exposures and still get a good percentage of good pictures.

Being a professional photographer I am perhaps prejudiced about these small cameras. I definitely don't care for them, principally because contact prints are of little interest when the original is so small. They must be enlarged to be of much value. When the negative is absolutely perfect as to selection of subject, exposure, and development, one can get a fair enlargement up to 5" x 7", but above that, the resulting enlargement is invariably flat. I have seen some fair 8" x 10" enlargements that the owner was very proud of. They were good, however, only because of the fact that they were freaks—that is, every condition had fortunately been correct. Had the same pictures been taken by a 2¼" x 2½" or a 2¼" x 3¼", the contacts would have been interesting and the 8" x 10" enlargements would have been snappier and much more pleasing.

When any negative is enlarged many times its original size, it enlarges the grain in proportionate size, and while the new "Panatomic" emulsions have very little grain, they do have some. Now an overexposed negative is grainier than a perfectly exposed one, so you can see my point. Take a hypothetical example of a negative one inch square, another two inches square. It will be seen that in making enlargement five inches square of each, the grain on the smaller negative will be enlarged just four times as much as the grain on the larger one; consequently, the enlargement from the two-inch negative will be less grainy, hence more pleasing to the eye.

Here in the American Museum of Natural History, where I am writing, I find several of these "Minnie" cameras. Dr. Robert Cushman Murphy recommends these miniature cameras for documentary records in natural history work. As he points out, he can use the small cameras quickly as a supplement to his other photographic records. But this fact must be borne in mind. If you have a "Minnie" negative that is not perfect—if it is over-exposed or under-exposed, you simply cannot get a pleasing enlargement; while, if you have a roll of 2¼" x 2½", or larger, with the identical range of exposure, you can get good enlargements from negatives that are not perfect. And I have yet to see anyone who can get a large percentage of perfect negatives in the high tropics where conditions vary so much that the exposure changes are more complicated than at any other place on earth. There is no doubt about this—*that the less a negative need be enlarged, the more pleasing the picture.* And again I say, try for a good picture rather than a perfect one; Africa is no place to experiment. Do that at home where you can get the picture over again if you miss. If you miss in Africa, the chances are that you will not be able to get the same picture again.

I shall conclude my remarks on miniature cameras by compromising. If you have one of these cameras, take it along, but please take a larger size for your more important subjects.

For many years my favorite still camera has been a 5" x 7", because in the early days all emulsions were grainy, but during the past few years the grain has been reduced to such an extent that I now find that with a 3¼" x 4¼" negative, I can enlarge as much and with quality as good as I used to get with 5″ x 7″. On my future expeditions I will use this size exclusively.

Use "Panatomic" film. Its emulsion keeps well, is panchromatic, and has such fine grain that it makes better enlargements than any other emulsion.

However, a Kodak is not suitable for long distance wild animal work. For this purpose I recommend the revolving back, series D Graflex, making pictures 3¼″ x 4¼″. Equipped with the f.2.9 Anastigmat lens, it has remarkable brilliancy in focusing. It is possible to get so much light on the ground glass with the diaphragm wide open that perfect focusing is simple. Then, cut down to the proper exposure, it gives the utmost in definition. This lens is ten times as fast as f.8 and is ideal for use in practically all weather. With it I recommend a 14″ f.4.5 telephoto lens. Such an outfit will photograph natives, scenery, game on the plains, and all the different species of wild animals.

I have found that for my work the Speed Graphic type of camera is well adapted, due to the speed with which it can be put to work and to its all-around efficiency. While this camera does not have the reflex advantage of the Graflex mentioned above, it has the same Graflex Focal Plane Shutter, and its compactness supplies a useful and desirable convenience. Both the Speed Graphic and the Revolving Back Series D Graflex make available the advantages of interchangeable lenses and the accommodation of a variety of photographic emulsions. On my next trip I plan to use both of the above cameras in the 3¼″ x 4¼″ size. Where pictures are to be made from air, I wish to recommend the Folmer Graflex K-10 Aero Camera, which has served me well in a variety of applications, which include many ground shots as well as those taken from planes.

One filter is enough for the inexperienced photographer—a K 1. It does not cut down the exposure to any appreciable extent, gives ample color correction to make good pictures, and will give good cloud effects without making them conspicuous. If you are an advanced photographer with experience in using a wider range of filters, take them along. But the average person is likely to make incorrect exposures with color filters of different grades.

Now a word about exposure meters. Of course, as far as most 16 mm. cameras are concerned, I have never considered them necessary, because the markings on the front of these cameras, if followed, are sufficient to result in good exposures. The fact remains, however, that a very large number of amateurs are using these meters for both stills and movies, and swear by them. To those who are not professional, these meters will be of value.

Any good, rigid tripod will do. Several makes are now on the market. I use them with "tilt" and "pan" attachments even for my still cameras as their use makes it possible to level and get perfect composition in much less time than when using tripods without the "tilt" and "pan" head.

With emulsions of such good keeping qualities it is no longer necessary to develop in the field. In Nairobi there are three good photographic stores—one an American, one German, and one English, besides several studios. They all do good work and 16 mm. film can be processed by two of the firms.

If you have the opportunity to send your films into Nairobi from time to time while you are in the field I would suggest that you do so, as it is a fact that the more quickly you can develop your negatives after exposure the more brilliant and snappy they are.

I will not go into details regarding guns or safari clothing or camp equipment. Use the guns you like best. If you are going after the very big game, use a .470 or .465; if smaller big game, use a Springfield, 9.3, .375 or any gun of similar caliber, and a shotgun. If you have your own guns take them along; if not, you can buy or rent them in Nairobi, where you can also obtain the best brands of ammunition.

You would be foolish to take safari clothing from here. In Nairobi or almost any East or Central African town, you can have the clothing best suited for the country made up overnight, reasonable as to cost, too, and the same applies to safari boots.

Several Nairobi merchants make excellent tents and all equipment for camp life. In fact, a person need take nothing except the clothing he would ordinarily wear when traveling anywhere. In Nairobi the same clothing is worn as would be in London or New York.

In Nairobi can be found, also, cameras and kodaks of every American and European make, but I recommend taking your cameras from here as this assures proper lens fitting, etc., and also allows you to become familiar with them on the way. I would also carry film and plates from here as you are assured of fresher stock. The Nairobi dealers must carry such a wide range of sizes that it is impossible for them to carry a large stock of every size, although you are practically sure of finding the common sizes.

I am often asked about the safari white hunters. This I cannot answer as that would seem to show favoritism. However, be sure you have a recognized white hunter; there are ten or fifteen of them in Nairobi. There are also many more who call themselves white hunters and are not—men who have drifted into the business without ample experience. A good, reliable, and experienced white hunter is very essential, for one's choice in this regard may make or break your safari. They know the seasons and where the game is most likely to be at the time you are there (game migrates to a great extent with the seasons). They have on their staffs the best gun bearers, headmen, cooks, porters, etc. They are perfect shots to stand by you in case of danger; they understand outfitting a safari so that you will have the best of equipment, foods, etc. And above all, they are delightful companions; their stories around the campfire make your safari something to remember.

I do not recommend employing white hunters through the tourist or travel agencies in this country. I *do* recommend that you book your passage through such an agency, for their facilities on the way out are valuable and most of them have representatives in Nairobi. I have found, however, that sometimes through the pressure of business they will employ for you the kind of white hunter who is not the most desirable, for the old, reliable white hunters book most of their safaris themselves. The best way to handle this matter is to write to the Hon. Secretary, East African Professional Hunters Association, Box 881, Nairobi, Kenya Colony.

Other matters can be taken up through the American Consulate in Nairobi and the Game Department in Nairobi. The Nairobi Game Department will give you full details regarding shooting licenses, etc., in Uganda and Tanganyika, as well as in Kenya.

To reach East Africa from America, there are a number of pleasant routes—direct from New York City to Cape Town by the American South African Line; from there fly up to Nairobi in four days by the Imperial Airways, or transship and go up the East Coast to Mombasa. Or you may go from New York to any of the Mediterranean cities by the American Export Line or by the Italian lines. If you proceed to Alexandria, Egypt, you can catch one of the Imperial Airways planes and be in Nairobi in three days. Or you can go across the Atlantic to London and catch one of the big Imperial Airways planes and be in Nairobi in six days. This company maintains an office in the Plaza Hotel, New York City.

As this book is finished, Osa and I are preparing to leave again for another glorious adventure, from which we hope to bring you another book and even better and bigger movies of wild animals and wild people.